# THE THEATRE AUDITION BOOK

## Playing Monologs from Contemporary, Modern, Period, Shakespeare and Classical Plays

## GERALD LEE RATLIFF

D0376888

MERIWETHER
Colorado Springs, Colorado

Meriwether Publishing Ltd., Publisher
P.O. Box 7710
Colorado Springs, CO 80933

Editor: Arthur L. Zapel
Typesetting: Elisabeth Hendricks
Cover design: Janice Melvin

**Library of Congress Cataloging-in-Publication Data**

Ratliff, Gerald Lee.
    The theatre audition book : playing monologs from contemporary, modern, period, Shakespeare, and classical plays / edited by Gerald Lee Ratliff. -- 1st ed.
        p.     cm.
    ISBN 1-56608-044-4 (pbk.)
    1. Monologues   2. Acting--Auditions   3. Drama   I. Title.
    PN2080.R39   1998
    808.82'45--dc21                      98-29131
                                                 CIP

2   3   4   5   6   7        03   02   01   00   99

# CONTENTS

## Chapter Four
### PLAYING SHAKESPEARE MONOLOGS ................................77

## Chapter Five
### PLAYING PERIOD MONOLOGS .......................................109

**Chapter Seven**
# PLAYING "NON-DRAMATIC" MONOLOGS ....................179

# ACKNOWLEDGMENTS

Excerpt from *Long Day's Journey into Night* by Eugene O'Neill. Copyright © 1953 by Yale University Press. Reprinted by permission of Yale University Press. All rights strictly reserved. All inquiries should be addressed to Yale University Press, 302 Temple Street, P.O. Box 209040, New Haven, Connecticut 06520.

Excerpt from *The Elephant Man* by Bernard Pomerance. Copyright © 1979 by Bernard Pomerance. All rights strictly reserved. Reprinted by permission of Alan Brodie Representation, Ltd. All inquiries should be addressed to Alan Brodie Representation, Ltd., 211 Piccadilly, London, W1V, 9LD, England.

Excerpt from *Tango* by Slawomir Mrozek. Translated by Ralph Manheim and Teresa Dzieduscycha. Copyright © 1968 by Grove Press. All rights strictly reserved. Reprinted by permission of Grove/Atlantic, Inc. Inquiries should be directed to Grove/Atlantic, Inc., 841 Broadway, New York, New York 10003.

Excerpt from *The Cavern* by Jean Anouilh. Translation copyright © 1966 by Jean Anouilh and Lucienne Hill. Copyright renewed © 1994 by Lucienne Hill. Reprinted by permission of Hill and Wang, a division of Farrar, Straus & Giroux, Inc.

Excerpt from *Luther* by John Osborne. All rights reserved. Reprinted by permission of Helen Osborne. Inquiries related to performance rights should be addressed to the author's agent Gordon Dickerson, 2 Crescent Grove, London, SW4, 7AH, England.

Excerpt from *The Typists* by Murray Schisgal. Copyright © 1963, renewed 1991 by Murray Schisgal. Reprinted by permission of International Creative Management, Inc. Published by Coward-McCann Contemporary Drama. CAUTION: Professionals and amateurs are hereby warned that *The Typists* is subject to a royalty. It is fully protected under the copyright laws of the United States of America, and of all countries covered by the International Copyright Union (including the Dominion of Canada and the rest of the British Commonwealth), and of all countries covered by the Pan-American Copyright Convention and the Universal Copyright Convention, and of all countries with which the United States has reciprocal copyright relations. All rights, including professional, amateur, motion picture, recitation, lecturing, public reading, radio broadcasting, television, and the rights of translation into foreign language are strictly reserved. Particular emphasis is laid on the question of readings, permission for which must be secured in writing. All inquiries (except for amateur rights in the United States and Canada) should be addressed to International Creative Management, 40 West 57th Street, New York, New York 10019. The amateur acting rights of *The Typists* are controlled exclusively by the Dramatists Play Service, Inc., 440 Park Avenue South, New York, New York 10016. No amateur performance of this play may be given without obtaining in advance the written permission of the Dramatists Play Service, Inc., and paying the requisite fee.

Excerpt from *I Hate Hamlet* by Paul Rudnick. All rights reserved. Reprinted by permission of the author. CAUTION: All amateur and professional stage performance

ix

# PREFACE

A number of interesting principles are at work in this handbook of audition practices and monolog performances. First, chapters one and two present a "blueprint" for preparing auditions and selecting audition materials to achieve distinction and individuality in performance. Second, the monologs selected for audition performance are conveniently grouped in historical "periods" from the classical to the contemporary. Third, chapter seven is a collection of interesting "non-dramatic" monologs adapted or edited from sources other than theatre playscripts that should challenge your skills in interpretation and characterization. Finally, there are a number of valuable resource materials that include selected readings, a survey of period dates, and a glossary of useful audition terms.

There is also a fundamental performance principle in the book that it is important to be an inventive, imaginative actor in the audition. The initial challenge, therefore, is to cultivate the critical skills needed to read a playscript with a keen and discerning eye; and to pay special attention to the essential details needed for a studied investigation of the dramatic and theatrical elements inherent in each selected monolog. The guidelines and strategies suggested in the introductory chapters on audition expectations should enrich your individual, self-expressive audition style and help promote fresh, original character portraits in performance.

The monologs selected for each historical period are representative of the competitive material you might expect to discover at auditions. Remember, however, that it is necessary to read the complete playscript for each selection before an audition in order to determine the special context in which the monolog reveals a character's intention, motivation, or point of view in the isolated moment of time, place, and action being described. It is also important to assume an audition performance attitude that concentrates on the "present" moment and embraces the monolog character as if you were playing the role for the first time.

Although each monolog includes a brief character analysis, you should isolate the primary motivating forces that appear to drive the monolog character to accomplish fundamental goals and objectives. Be attentive as well to the distinctive features and suggestive subtext of each monolog character in order to promote imaginative audition performance approaches that reinforce your own personal, unmistakable personality. Once you have discovered your own performance image to communicate the monolog character portrait, strive continuously to maintain the authenticity and the honesty of that image at every rehearsal and in the audition.

Finally, with experience and the practical knowledge gained through extensive audition performances you should be able to maintain a consistent blueprint that operates in a logical, systematic order that is most appropriate for your own individual skills and talents. The creative process that you devise in the rehearsal process, however, is never complete; and it will be important to remain open and flexible in your interpretation of each monolog character to appear fresh and spontaneous in the subsequent audition performance. Consider every audition performance as an occasion to gain the first-hand experience necessary to meet the changing and frequently unpredictable artistic challenges of the contemporary theatre. Constantly strive to increase the range and the depth of your audition performances, relying upon your basic instincts and individual self-expression to give voice and body to your monolog character portraits. This energy and enthusiasm should result in a persuasive expression of a finely etched audition performance!

Gerald Lee Ratliff
SUNY - Potsdam
January, 1998

# CHAPTER ONE
# PREPARING FOR AUDITIONS

*"Calm down! Only your whole career depends on this scene!"*
— Alfred Hitchcock, Film Director

Preparing for a successful audition involves much more than just a basic appreciation and understanding of playscript interpretation or performance technique. Long before actual audition notices are posted for public call, the director may have already begun to "see" and to "hear" the characters in the playscript and to think of the audition process as a simple, efficient device to discover who among the assembled actors most clearly resembles the director's own preconceived image — vocal and physical — of the stage figures being cast. This convenient approach to the audition process allows the director to review a large number of actors in a relatively brief period of time. In this respect, the audition is very similar to a job interview; except that in this particular case the actor is performing answers to the questions about the character(s) being asked by the director.

It is important, therefore, that the actor be familiar with the traditional audition process and be prepared for any unexpected audition demands. Because there are as many methods of conducting auditions as there are imaginative or demanding directors, the actor should become aware of the following types of auditions and the expectations associated with each type. The first type of audition is the *cold reading*, where the actor is given a prepared or "set" speech and asked to perform the selection with little or no time for preparation or thought related to interpretation and characterization. A number of directors use the cold reading approach to auditions to determine an actor's immediate talent in phrasing dialog, demonstrating initial interpretation skills, and in suggesting vocal and physical characterization.

The second type of audition is the *prepared reading*, where the actor performs two contrasting memorized monologs — usually one or two minutes each — from classical, Shakespeare, and modern or contemporary playscripts. A number of directors use the prepared reading approach to auditions to determine an actor's ability to distinguish different character attitudes or moods, to catalog actors by "type" for subsequent callbacks, or to evaluate the general level of potential talent available before pursuing the initial production concept.

There may be auditions which are *open*, and all interested actors are encouraged to attend; or auditions may be *closed*, and only those who have been invited attend. *General* auditions, for example, are the most common and may be used to screen actors for more intensive review at later, more structured audition sessions. Some auditions may also include *improvisation*, where the actor's imagination and inventiveness might be challenged in a series of impromptu or unscripted exercises and theatre games; and *directed readings*, where the director may give specific instructions in dialog interpretation, movement, or vocal/physical response for the actor to perform in a selected monolog or scene. Both improvisation and the directed reading approach to auditions allow the director to evaluate the actor's spontaneity, flexibility, and capability to follow direction.

Too many actors make an initial judgment error in failing to consider the type of the announced audition; and select monologs or scenes that they "like" or that are "well-known" without regard to the expectations of each type of audition. No small part of preparing for the audition is the selection of monologs or scenes that are appropriate and suitable to both the actor's talent and the director's casting need. Remember also, that the primary objective of any type of audition is for the actor to demonstrate a performance "personality" that is capable of achieving that vocal and physical character portrait the director has already begun to imagine as part of the production concept.

Perhaps that is why the audition, in many ways, needs to be even more inspired and inventive than playing a role in an actual production — if you are unable to meet the director's audition expectations in terms of voice, body, age, or range you may never have a later opportunity to deliver a stunning performance before a live audience! And that is why the actor should continue to polish skills in scene study, interpretation, and characterization by auditioning at every opportunity presented and under as many different circumstances as possible — television, community theatre, school plays, pageants, films, commercials, or staged readings.

## BASIC PRINCIPLES

The serious actor should know that there is more involved in the audition process than merely exhibiting imagination and spontaneous creativity. There must be careful analysis of the playscript and rehearsal exploration that provides the performance clues necessary to sketch a memorable character portrait in an audition. It is also important to review the following basic principles *before* selecting an audition monolog or scene.

- Auditions are generally limited to a total time period of three to four minutes for *two contrasting* selections.

- Auditions in professional theatre may rely upon an "interview" or a "resume review" to select actors for an invited reading.

- Some auditions may include a "sample scene" that actors must review in a brief time period of ten to fifteen minutes before performing the selection.

- Some auditions provide *sides*, or photocopied pages of selected scenes or speeches to be read, several days in advance of the posted audition call.

- If the audition specifically calls for a "classic" selection it usually means a *verse* monolog or scene.

- If the audition indicates an "interview" as part of the posted call this is a business appointment that requires formal, professional responses to questions usually asked by the director. Be attentive, alert, and enthusiastic — but avoid "chummy," too familiar, or personal questions.

• "Standard American" speech is an audition expectation and excellent diction is an audition rule. There should be no vocal regionalisms, colloquialisms, or distracting speech patterns. The use of accents should be limited and then only if accurate and authentic.

These basic principles are essential elements to consider when preparing for an audition. It is important, therefore, to be adaptable and flexible; rather than to develop a rigid performance blueprint structure that might be shattered if the actor is suddenly "cut off" by the director a few seconds into the audition! An adaptable and flexible approach to auditions suggests that the actor (1) Maintains a repertoire of several monologs and scenes that are appropriate for any type of audition performance. (2) Prepares for general auditions by reading the entire playscript, not just those scenes in which a favorite character appears. (3) Pays particular attention to cultivating audition material that promotes vocal variety, ease of movement, and emotional honesty.

## INITIAL STAGE FRIGHT

Perhaps the most difficult principle to address in preparing for the audition is the initial, inevitable "stage fright" that accompanies all performance situations — whether it is acting, speaking, dancing, singing, or any other public presentation. There are many popular theories about stage fright, and just as many professional opinions on ways to deal with it. Stage fright has been examined in depth by psychologists, who view it as a mental state of apprehension that precedes every public presentation event. It has been studied at length by communication teachers, who view it as a physical state of bodily anxiety that necessarily accompanies any performance or public speech activity. It has been reviewed by clinical researchers, who label it an emotional state of initial fear when facing an audience. In all fields of study, stage fright has been subject to intensive analysis and almost every conceivable test or measurement without revealing either its cause or its potential cure.

But stage fright is not difficult to describe. We have all experienced the basic symptoms in performance situations. It generally manifests

4

itself in nervousness and anxiety that affects the voice and the body. It is a discomforting and puzzling fear that makes us doubt our ability to speak or to move in public presentations. With experience and a positive attitude, however, we all learn how to combat the sweaty palms, knocking knees, and pounding heart that are associated with stage fright.

The first and most important principle to learn about stage fright is that it is *not* a personality defect that indicates we are inferior, inept, or incompetent in our public performances and presentations. A second important principle is that even the most seasoned performers or speakers continue to experience minor degrees of tension and nervousness when facing an audience. A third important principle is that stage fright may be a "learned" behavior, resulting from unpleasant or negative incidents and events early in life that make us dread appearing before an audience. A fourth, and final, important principle related to stage fright is that it can be a *positive* experience which, when harnessed, gives our public performances or presentations animation and vitality!

The beginning actor, especially in the audition process, must begin to address the phantom of stage fright by understanding how it affects performance and what imaginative strategies are available to combat its symptoms. A good starting point is to consider every public situation — whether it is an oral report, address, social meeting, or lecture — as an occasion to combat stage fright, and to develop lifelong learning skills that may lead to effective, tension-free communication with any audience. Actively seek to participate in public activities which cultivate a voice that is pleasant and resonant, and a body that is relaxed and flexible. Indeed, the more the actor can actively participate in performance-related activities, the easier it will be to exhibit a comfortable, mature portrait or poise and self-confidence in an audition.

Since improvement in any performance situation must proceed with some specific guidelines, now is the time to take a personal inventory of your behavior and personality under stress and strain. Begin where more experienced actors have begun (1) With an analysis of those particular facial expressions or gestures that surface when you feel insecure. (2) With an evaluation of those distracting bodily actions that emerge when you are nervous. (3) With a survey of anxiety-induced habits such as scratching the head or blinking the eyes when you are distracted or fearful. Once you have become aware of your "automatic" responses or reactions to public performance or presentation situations, you should be able to more effectively identify such distracting mannerisms and enhance your image as a confident and capable public performer.

Just knowing what to expect can be a first step forward in learning to control stage fright. For example, the actor can anticipate a cracking voice, dry throat, rapid breathing, weak knees, shaking hands, "tongue twisting," and a sick stomach in beginning audition performances. Now, when the actor expects the voice to be "cracking" or "scratchy" it is possible to concentrate on specific vocal exercises that will free it from stress and strain. When the actor expects the body to be "shaking" or "weak" it is possible to identify specific physical exercises that will relax it from initial anxiety and tension.

That is why it is important to learn as much as possible about stage fright. When you arm yourself with the facts and know how stage fright expresses itself in the audition situation, you should be better prepared to deal with it calmly and directly. Although all performers experience similar reactions to stage fright, we are all individuals. It is important, therefore, to anticipate your unique vocal and physical responses; and to be able to invent personal strategies to combat your own audition performance needs. Once you have gained audition experience and begin to know your individual strengths and weaknesses, you should also begin to develop your own creative, personal exercises to promote a sense of relaxation and self-confidence in performance. Of course, you will still need to be familiar with other vocal and physical exercises; but you are the person to determine what works best in the audition performance. Here are some strategies by recent student performers who gained experience and self-confidence in the audition process and whose individual, unique approaches to combating stage fright were both inventive and imaginative.

- "The important thing to remember is that you are not on trial — just *do* it!"

- "Taking yourself out of a present-tense situation and practicing deep breathing techniques will ultimately lessen apprehension."

- "Going for an easy run a half-hour before the audition lessens my fear and nervousness."

- "I jump up and down, shake my hands, and wiggle my toes to relieve any pent-up anxiety or tension."

- "Say to yourself, 'Unless you calm down you'll faint and look like a real jerk!' "

- "Find your own 'inner space,' a deserted island, a mountain top, or a clearing in the forest — a secluded space where you can feel at peace with yourself."

These inventive and imaginative audition strategies should suggest to you that there are universal characteristics associated with a successful audition performance. First, success in the audition performance is the direct result of self-confidence and poise. Second, the successful performer is able to control tension and nervousness so that it does not interfere with the audition performance. Third, the experienced performer gains self-confidence and self-respect when thoroughly prepared and relaxed. Fourth, actors need to maintain an active catalog of relaxation exercises to prepare themselves for audition performance; sometimes using mental or physical exercises like jogging or visualization. Fifth, the more audition experience the actor gains in performance, the easier it is to transfer initial apprehension and anxiety from the present-tense situation to a less threatening one — like finding your own "inner space" or practicing deep breathing techniques.

The important point to keep in mind in your own unique approach to audition performance — to quote Theodore Roosevelt, who learned about stage fright firsthand in his early, youthful political campaigns and later, mature public presentations — is that:

"Any beginner is apt to have 'buck fever' the first time. What you need is not courage, but nerve control, cool headedness. This you can get only by actual practice. It is very largely a matter of habit, in the sense of repeated exercise of willpower. If you have the right stuff, you will grow stronger and stronger with each exercise of it."

Of course, we are all more severe on ourselves when we lack significant confidence in our ability to "perform" before an audience; especially when that audience appears as a sea of strange faces! But the truth, as you will soon discover as your own confidence and poise grows in audience performance, is that *all* performers and public speakers initially begin as awkward, timid novices. Once they gain valuable experience, however, they suddenly emerge as dynamic and persuasive actors or orators; capable of appearing animated, mature, and poised before any audience!

Unfortunately, "stage fright" has become a convenient password for some unprepared actors whose audition material lacks vivid, incisive character portraits; or whose audition performance is marred by imperfect speech, slurring words, forgetting lines of dialog, or appearing stiff and rigid in movement. While all of these stage fright symptoms have the potential to disrupt an audition performance, the serious performer must consider some of the more realistic and practical reasons a director may choose not to cast an actor.

- The actor did not adequately display the emotional, intellectual, physical, or vocal range needed for the character portrait.

- The actor did not adequately meet the director's pre-conceived notion of the imagined character's height, weight, or age.

- The actor's interpretation of the role did not adequately capture the director's perception of the imagined character's attitude, mood, or temperament.

8

• The actor's personality did not appear to be compatible with the other performers being considered for the ensemble.

There may, of course, have been other reasons for the director to have cast another potential performer; and it is important for the actor to discover these reasons in order to be more successful in subsequent audition situations. It would be appropriate, therefore, to ask the director — once the final cast has been posted — for a professional assessment of the audition performance. Of special interest should be an evaluation of

• The actor's material selected for the audition.

• The actor's vocal and physical range.

• The actor's movement.

• The actor's interpretation of the role.

• The actor's performance technique.

• The actor's emotional and intellectual range

• Or any "problem areas" that might need an immediate address.

Recently, there has also been a movement toward non-traditional casting which has influenced some directors in their decision-making. Non-traditional approaches cast actors in roles which, in past theatre practices, might not have been considered appropriate, and which are color-blind, with no casting preference to race, gender, or ethnicity. Non-traditional casting may be conceptual, and the director may choose to change the race, gender, or ethnicity of a selected character in order to suggest an innovative or new interpretation of a playscript. Non-traditional casting may also feature performance opportunities for trained or untrained performers who are physically challenged in hearing, speaking, seeing, or moving capabilities.

Striking examples of non-traditional casting might include the recent Whoopi Goldberg role of the comic Greek slave, traditionally played by a male, in the musical revival of *A Funny Thing Happened on the Way to the Forum*; the role of a hearing-impaired young woman in *Children of a Lesser God* being played by the hearing-impaired actress Marlee Matlin; HIV-positive actors being cast in playscripts that describe the AIDS crisis, like in *The Baltimore Waltz, The Normal Heart,* or *Whose Life Is It Anyway?*; or the physically challenged being cast in leading roles in playscripts that are concerned with social issues of disability, like in *The Miracle Worker* or *The Elephant Man.* All of these examples should be kept in mind when considering the principles of non-traditional casting currently in practice; and to be prepared, emotionally as well as intellectually, for the inevitable rejection that is a realistic part of the audition process.

## AUDITION ETIQUETTE

In order to familiarize yourself with some of the special features associated with audition etiquette, please review the following practices to enhance your competitive edge in performance. Although you will no doubt learn much more about audition etiquette through experience, the basic principles listed below should guide you in constructing an audition routine that gives meaning and vitality to your performance.

### AUDITION TIME

Always anticipate arriving early for an audition — and never arrive late. Think of the audition time as an appointment and be punctual and prepared. If there should be an unexpected delay or an emergency, it is the actor's professional responsibility to call the theatre and inform the staff of the delay. Although the old theatre slogan "Hurry up ... and then wait your turn!" remains very much in practice for all auditions, learn to budget your time wisely. Review your monologs while you wait your turn to audition; and don't forget to leave sufficient time for warm-up vocal and physical exercises. It might also be a good idea to budget some time for personal reflection on your goals and objectives in the audition — assuming an audition attitude that is concerned with simplicity and subtlety as though the character were being played for the first time. Concentrate only on the present and focus all of your energy and thought on the action and the dialog of the monolog(s) that are part of the audition performance. Avoid the tendency to socialize at auditions, and show respect for your fellow actors by keeping noise, disruption, and distraction to a minimum. Remember that you have a limited amount of time to give distinction and individuality to the audition performance, so time management is essential for success!

### AUDITION WARDROBE

An appropriate, suggestive audition wardrobe that indicates the time period of the playscript or the mood and attitude of the character reflects an understanding of both the selected monolog and the chosen character. Street make-up for women is appropriate, and hair may be worn up for classical roles, but always away from the face so expressions may be clearly seen. Men may experiment with growing simple mustaches, sideburns, or period hair styles if they are essential to the character portrait being etched in the audition. A light, warm bronzer is also appropriate for men. The audition wardrobe should be carefully selected in terms of cut, style, and color to highlight the

actor's physical dimensions. Avoid the tendency to wear theatrical costumes to the audition, and do not rely on accessories such as wigs, swords, hats, jewelry, platform shoes, or elaborate hand props that might be distracting in performance. Remember that the audition wardrobe should subtly reveal a character's personality, idio-syncrasies, or taste in fashion, as well as record a character's lifestyle, occupation, or sense of self. It is also essential to carefully select an audition wardrobe that makes appropriate use of

traditional designer principles of line, mass, color, texture, and ornament to give added dimension to character and to highlight individuality.

## AUDITION FORMS

The audition form, or try-out sheet, needs to be filled in completely and honestly. It is especially important to indicate both home and work telephone numbers, and don't forget to list all potential conflicts, like work hours, regularly scheduled appointments, classes, or any other standing obligations that might occur during the announced rehearsal, production, or performance dates. It is also important to indicate you are able to reschedule any listed conflicts if cast. In listing experience, include the complete title of the playscript, specific name of the character role played, and the theatre company where the production was staged. Be honest in your description of any roles played and in any "specialties" you might have like juggling, mime, stage combat, jazz, or modern dance. You should also make some mention of any musical instruments played or any novelty skills like magic tricks, circus techniques, or impersonations. Some audition forms may ask if you are currently taking any acting, dancing, or singing lessons with a professional instructor so be prepared to indicate the specific area of intensive study, number of years studied, and name and address of the professional instructor. Remember that the audition form is similar to the job application form, so suit your response to the specific request — and be direct and honest in your description!

## AUDITION SPACE

Although some actors apparently give very little thought to the location of the performance, a thorough preparation should include a review of the audition space. If possible, visit the announced theatre location before the scheduled audition time; paying particular attention to the size of the stage, rehearsal spaces, entrance and exit doorways, seating arrangement, and acoustical sounds. Rehearsal in the audition space should reveal the vocal and physical demands of performance, as well as the size and scope of gestures or movement in relationship to the dimensions of the playing area. Familiarity with the audition space should help promote a comfortable and relaxed atmosphere in which to execute fluid and natural movement. Knowing first-hand the demands and limitations of the audition space should also promote an attractive vocal quality that allows the actor to effectively highlight and punctuate important character attitudes, ideas, or moods. A careful review of the playing space should further help the actor combat the initial anxiety and tension frequently associated with public performance in an unfamiliar environment, and it is excellent preparation when having to determine the degree to tone down an audition performance or the degree of intimacy, naturalness, and subtlety appropriate for the given circumstances of the monolog or scene and the physical dimensions of the playing area.

## ADDITIONAL DIMENSIONS

There are a number of additional dimensions to consider in preparing for the audition, and it is very important to approach the audition in a calm, relaxed manner rather than as a hectic cattle call with other equally prepared and talented performers. Remember that the performance audition involves considerable pre-planning in terms of selecting memorable monologs or scenes, selecting an appropriate wardrobe, pursuing a disciplined rehearsal schedule, and composing a well-written and professional resume. All of these preliminary elements are essential ingredients that will give distinction and individuality to an audition so be metic-

ulous and precise in your preparation.

From the director's perspective, an additional dimension of the audition is discovering actors who are at ease in the interpretation of the role(s) they are playing, and who demonstrate a marked flexibility in voice/body, a natural or conversational delivery of dialog lines, or an intellectual and emotional range of character understanding. The director is also concerned with discovering actors who may exhibit spontaneity, stage presence, movement style, and inventive phrasing in character interpretation.

Some directors may use the audition performance to look for compatible pairs of actors — either contrasts or similarities — as well as the spirit and spark of an ensemble in making final casting decisions. In this respect, the director's perspective on additional dimensions for the audition performance may include type casting or casting against type. Type casting involves the selection of actors whose age, height, weight, ethnic look, physique, personality, or attitude most closely resembles the director's own interpretation of the character role. Casting against type involves the selection of actors whose size, age, physical appearance, or performance style and technique are the exact opposite of what the character role appears at first glance to suggest. The practice of casting against type is, of course, especially prevalent in film; with notable examples including Jack Nicholson as The Joker in *Batman*, Madonna in the title role of *Evita*, and Gary Sinise in the biographical *Truman*. When motivated by critical insight and a creative interpretation, the director's use of type casting or casting against type may result in sparkling character portraits that are inspired and incisive.

From the actor's perspective, significant additional dimensions of the audition include the preparation of supplementary materials like supporting letters of recommendation, professional photographs, and the performance resume. For those auditions which specifically request supporting letters of recommendation, the actor should maintain a current file of reference letters that can easily and quickly be photocopied and forwarded in advance to the theatre representative identified to receive them. Prospective letters of recommendation should be solicited from recent agents, directors, producers, or teachers who know the candidate well. The written letters of recommendation should offer critical commentary on a number of significant issues including the candidate's ability to take stage direction, to work as a member of the ensemble, to function under pressure, to meet rehearsal deadlines, and to make a positive contribution to the production. Supporting letters of recommendation should also comment on the actor's rehearsal attitude, maturity, personality, and special skills that might enrich a production. It is very important for supporting reference letters to call specific attention to the candidate's sense of professionalism, responsibility, and leadership qualities.

The actor should choose potential references as carefully as audition monologs are selected; paying particular attention to references who give a representative view of skills and talents. The selected references should offer a variety of professional and personal assessments of the candidate and paint the recommendation upon a broad canvas of intimate knowledge that allows a well-drawn self-portrait to emerge. It is always a good idea for the actor to request a copy of the recommendation before it is forwarded to the designated theatre representative; or to collect appropriate letters of recommendation in a placement bureau file and have them sent directly to the requesting theatre representative.

A final additional dimension for the actor to consider in preparing for the audition is the professional photograph and performance resume. The professional photograph is generally a current black-and-white 8"x10" head shot. The photograph should reveal the actor in an informal, natural pose wearing subtle makeup, light-colored shirt or blouse, and having cut, trimmed hair. Avoid photographs that are highly theatrical or artificially posed. The photograph should be well-lit with limited shadowing; and accessories like costume jewelry, ear or nose rings, and glitter should be eliminated. The photograph should also reveal a modest open-neck exposure that is appropriate for a relaxed pose. Some actors choose to submit a character photograph as well, but an increasing number of casting agents and directors prefer to initially view the actor in a more subtle photograph rather than to witness a highly stylized, transformed portrait with excessive makeup, false hair, and character rubber nose! In choosing a photographer, make sure that you shop around to compare prices and quality of prints. The photographer should share samples of the theatre head shots on file and should quote a specific price for a specific number of prints. It is always a good idea to interview a prospective photographer and to schedule some preliminary head shots for review before making a final order commitment.

The performance resume that is part of most audition procedures is also 8"x10" and should be stapled or attached with rubber cement to the backside of the professional photograph. Think of the performance resume as a thumbnail autobiographical sketch that includes the essential information a director would need to know in making an informed casting decision. Information to be detailed on the performance resume includes the actor's complete name and mailing address; home and business phone number; height, weight, and age range; color of hair and eyes; and vocal singing range. In listing previous experience, place the most current credits first (high school, college/university, community, or professional); and indicate the specific categories in terms of the name of the character played, the playscript, and the theatre in which the production was staged. The performance resume may also include brief categories that include "honors and awards," "activities," "special skills," or "professional training." It is important that the performance resume include reference to special skills like musical instruments played or foreign languages spoken, and the listing of professional training talents like sports, juggling, mime, or modern dance should be added if appropriate.

The professional photograph and the autobiographical performance resume are essential ingredients when anticipating an audition; and the actor should be as careful and conscientious in the preparation of these supporting documents as in the time spent on rehearsal for the audition. Make sure that all of your supporting written materials are of high quality, free of typographical or grammatical errors, and neatly printed or photocopied on bonded paper. Remember that the director's first impression may not be your audition performance; it may actually be a review of your written supporting materials submitted before the audition!

## MUSICAL THEATRE

Although preparing for the musical theatre try-out is very similar to the traditional audition, there are a number of distinct differences that the actor needs to review. The general characteristics of the American musical comedy plot, or storyline, is often quite different from a standard theatre playscript in the absence of description, narration, or detail that reveals the development of character. There are also fewer complications, reversals, and recognition scenes that clarify character moods and attitudes. In addition, the plot of musicals frequently has the following general characteristics that distinguish it from the standard theatre storyline.

- The opening scene of a musical introduces the principal character(s) and establishes the inherent conflict of personality or thought that must be resolved in the later development of the plot.

- The storyline is primarily simple and highlights individual or ensemble songs rather than complicated exchanges of dialog.

- Dialog and lyrics are clear and precise, and rely on images to convey the thought, mood, or emotion of the moment.

- The plot is embellished by elaborate ensemble songs, reprises, and dances that frame the main action of the characters.

- Musicals inherently underplay the psychological or intellectual exploration of character development and concentrate primarily upon expressing the emotional content of a character's attitude or mood.

Although musical theatre characters may sometimes appear superficial, an attempt is still made to present vivid, incisive portraits that mirror reality. As a consequence, it is possible to hear — in both dialog and song — characters performing heroic deeds, making ignorant blunders, exhibiting both courage and cowardice, committing errors in judgment or displaying basic emotions such as anger, frustration, or greed.

By paying attention to the songs of the musical, you should notice that characters emerge stronger from facing the obstacles they see as limiting their potential success. Another clue can be gained from observing the pattern of suffering or despair so common in musicals. Look for the honesty and frankness in the songs of your character; and note how the lyrics help to reflect the character's basic nature and disposition.

One of the most challenging responsibilities in preparing for the musical theatre audition is to interpret the character objectively as a means of shedding light on the theme of the musical. It is also important in musical theatre interpretation to learn the art of "acting a song." A traditional theatre scene is considerably longer than a musical theatre song, and timing is the key to musical interpretation. You must learn to speak in the tempo of the song and to voice lines on pitch. Remember also that most musicals have a poetic lyric, and that you must act several beats in advance of what you are speaking or singing.

In approaching a song in the audition performance, it is helpful to know the motivation and dramatic intent of the song, to whom it is being sung, where the action of the song and the scene is taking place, and what subtext is revealed in the song. It is useful to copy the song lyrics in a looseleaf notebook and to approach the rehearsal of the song just as you might work on a traditional theatre monolog or scene. Also consider the role that facial expressions, gestures, movement, emotional responses, or physical reactions might play in giving dimension and scope to your musical character interpretation.

Most musical theatre auditions require two contrasting songs (ballad and show tune) to be sung in your own *singing* range and a novelty or specialty number that features your *vocal* range. The time limit is usually two to three minutes total, and many actors edit potential audition songs to eight to ten bars of the most memorable lyrics. For general auditions, maintaining a song repertoire that includes eight to sixteen measures from at least four contrasting songs would be sufficient to indicate singing and vocal range. The specialty song should be carefully selected to highlight your musical theatre personality and individual signature. All potential audition songs should showcase your ability to vocalize mood, tempo, phrasing, and technique.

Show songs written directly for stage performance and revealing complex characterization or dramatic content are especially valuable audition material to display emotional quality or intensity. Voicing show songs rather than folk, pop, or rock promotes the dramatic rather than the technical demands of a score, and encourages more three-dimensional characterization in the audition performance. It is also a good performance idea to avoid audition songs that have been popularized by well-known personalities or audition songs that have become closely identified with individual or group star singers.

The musical theatre audition will no doubt include dance preparation that may be an additional ingredient in final casting decision-making. The audition dance element usually requires learning a combination number of jazz, ballet, or tap in a large group of performers (fifteen to twenty) and then repeating the combination in smaller groups (five to seven) for the audition performance. The primary objective of the dance audition is to evaluate the actor's ability to execute a pattern of movement set to music and to demonstrate fluid and expressive dance steps. It is very important, therefore, that the actor's preparation for the dance audition include relaxation exercises that explore tension-free body alignment and natural, expressive movement. In addition, if there is an audition call for chorus members, you may anticipate preparation that includes a maximum of sixteen bars from a selected song or one solo song of two to three minutes that demonstrates your vocal range.

As you begin your musical theatre audition preparation, it is appropriate to work closely with an experienced *vocal coach* rather than a *voice teacher.* The more experienced vocal coach should be able to provide useful direction and guidance in performance approaches to discover character intentions or motivations, analyze song lyrics, project vocal intensity and honesty, select audition songs, suggest character interpretation and subtext, or stage potential audition songs. An experienced vocal coach should be able to cultivate your understanding of the need to think of the audition song as an acting opportunity — one that vocally reveals a three-dimensional characterization in its effective use of attitude, mood, and phrasing to reveal a memorable character portrait.

It is also important to consider the performance role that facial expressions, pauses, and physical reactions might play in giving added dimension and depth to your sung interpretation of the selected audition character. Finally, a musical theatre characterization is a creative way to fill the empty space in musicals when performers stand full-front stage center to sing directly to the audience. Imagine the song as a scene between you and another invisible acting partner. Direct your attention toward the audience, move with poise and grace, and exhibit the self-confidence and vitality that help to display your physical as well as vocal talents.

## Summary

Preparing for the audition is the most crucial step in the actor's preliminary approach to performance. It involves a familiarity with audition procedures as well as expectations associated with each type of audition performance. Each actor's blueprint for an audition performance should include a review of the basic principles related to selecting appropriate monologs or scenes, meeting time limits for audition materials, and the special demands of audition interviews, improvisations, or staged readings.

Each actor's personal blueprint for an audition performance must pay attention to the initial stage fright that accompanies all public presentations, and should include creative strategies or exercises that address the common, distracting symptoms of stage fright. There is also a responsibility of the actor to learn from the audition process and to begin to understand — and to accept — some of the considerations like non-traditional or type casting that may influence a director's decision-making.

Of special concern to the actor in preparing for the audition should be an awareness of the etiquette required for time, wardrobe, forms, and space. The initial preparation for the audition should also include an awareness of the additional dimensions involved in the director's casting perspective as well as those actor perspectives like supporting letters of recommendation, a professional photograph, and a performance resume.

Perhaps the best authorities on preparing for the audition are those seasoned actors who, through trial and error, gained first-hand experience of what is truly involved in an audition performance. The lessons learned, although painful in some instances, now point the way to the key element that distinguishes a memorable audition preparation and subsequent performance: *you must be a disciplined actor.* This implies not only a well-defined and orderly system of preparation for the audition, but also a selective approach to choosing appropriate audition monologs or scenes and an orderly audition rehearsal period as well.

Don't forget, as well, the special demands of a musical theatre audition and pay particular attention to acting a song as part of a three-dimensional vocal characterization. Learn to distinguish between your singing range and your vocal range, and look for show songs rather than folk, pop, or rock to promote the dramatic demands of a score. It will also be necessary to include dance preparation in your rehearsal period to demonstrate an ability to execute fluid patterns of movement and expressive dance steps needed to suggest a memorable character portrait. In summary, as an actor preparing for the audition, you must make sure that your disciplined approach is cohesive and consistent, and that it is flexible enough to permit the inspirational and inventive treasure chest of your own unique imagination and individual creativity to clearly emerge. The more your audition blueprint is memorable for its radiant aura of authenticity, spontaneity, and honesty, the more successful should be your audition performance. As you become better acquainted with your character in rehearsal, you may wish to include observation, informal discussion, and role models in your final audition performance blueprint. Use your preliminary preparation and rehearsal time wisely, making an outline or performance chart of the character's personality traits and thoughts as they are revealed in the selected monolog or scene. Remember also, that the audition performance is only given added dimension by your original invention, imagination, and interpretation. This essential ingredient of personal creativity requires a degree of risk-taking and uninhibited abandon in assuming the role of the character suggested in the monolog or scene, but when you are successful in your complex characterization the more vivid and memorable the audition performance is likely to be for the audience of spectators!

21

## SELECTED READINGS

The following suggested readings are recommended for the actor who may like to review the audition process in terms of both practice and principle. The readings provide additional information related to audition preparation and rehearsal techniques. There is also an effort made here to provide useful information related to audition expectations and a practical understanding of the traditional audition procedures.

Bartow, Arthur. *The Director's Voice: Twenty-One Interviews.* New York: Theatre Communications Group, 1988.

Cohen, Arthur. *Acting Professionally.* Mountain View, California: Mayfield Publishing Company, 1990.

Cole, Toby and Helen K. Chinoy. *Actors on Acting.* New York: Crown Books, 1980.

Craig, David. *A Performer Prepares.* New York: Applause Theatre Books, 1996.

Fridell, Squire. *Acting in Television Commercials for Fun and Profit.* New York: Crown Books, 1980.

Hay, Peter. *Broadway Anecdotes.* New York: Oxford University Press, 1989.

Hobgood, Burnet. *Master Teachers of Theatre.* Carbondale, Illinois. Southern Illinois University Press, 1988.

Hunt, Gordon. *How to Audition.* New York: Harper and Row Publishers, 1977.

Markus, Tom. *The Professional Actor.* New York: Drama Book Specialists, 1979.

Nagler, A. M. *Black Drama.* New York: Hawthorn Press, 1967.

Nahas, Rebecca. *Your Acting Career: How to Break Into and Survive in the Theatre.* New York: Crown Books, 1976.

Poggi, Jack. *The Monologue Workshop.* New York: Applause Theatre Books, 1996.

Shurtleff, Michael. *Audition.* New York: Bantam Books, 1980.

# CHAPTER TWO
# SELECTING AUDITION MATERIALS

*"Let those who cannot sense the magic threshold of the stage
not presume to cross it."*

— Stanislavski

In selecting potential materials for the audition, the actor should begin with careful research to discover the complexities of the playscript in terms of structure, language, and characterization so that a performance blueprint and staging possibilities for the selected monolog or scene may be explored in the rehearsal period. It is important, of course, to suit potential materials to the posted audition call — whether the call is for a specific character, specialty character, or a general character that is suitable to your own age, experience, vocal/physical range, or personality. Obviously, the first task in selecting materials for the audition is to suit the selected monolog or scene to the type of playscript or the role being cast in the production.

Beginning actors frequently select an unsuitable type of playscript or a character that is not appropriate in either style or period to the announced audition call. For example, an inexperienced, youthful actor selecting an audition monolog or scene featuring Shakespeare's older and more mature King Lear would be inappropriate for an announced call for the adolescent Romeo in Shakespeare's *Romeo and Juliet.* Likewise, in an announced audition call for Arthur Miller's aging sons in *Death of a Salesman,* it would be inappropriate for the actor to offer a verse monolog or scene of the younger adult character Haemon in the classical Greek playscript *Oedipus the King* by Sophocles.

When reviewing potential audition materials for the type of

playscript or the role being cast in the playscript, it is wise to keep in mind that if the announced playscript is written in verse and features a role similar to your own age, it would be most appropriate to select a complementary monolog or scene also written in verse and featuring a character who shares your own vocal/physical characteristics. Here are a number of other important considerations to keep in mind when attempting to match audition selections by type and character with the posted audition call.

- If auditioning for a playscript that is written in translation — like Molière's *The Miser*, Chekhov's *The Three Sisters*, or Ibsen's *Hedda Gabler* — make sure that you secure the same translation for rehearsal that is being used in the audition.

- If auditioning for a playscript that has a rather frequent or recent history of production, make sure that you secure the acting edition to prepare for the audition. The acting edition may include italicized stage directions or character performance clues used in the premier or revival production that would be useful information for your rehearsal and audition performance.

- If auditioning for a playscript that has a type and character similar to ones in which you have had previous stage experience, select a monolog or scene based upon your past performance(s) for the audition. You might also piece together a sequence of character speeches from your past performances — if the cutting and editing has a beginning, middle, and end — to use as audition material.

For most auditions, however, it will be necessary to select a potential playscript and read it in its entirety before selecting appropriate materials for the audition. At first, it is well to read the playscript appreciatively, with an ear for character interpretation and an eye for creative staging clues. The first reading should develop an indication of the character's intellectual and emotional thought(s), and should suggest whether the actor is sensitive to the character

24

description and given circumstances of the playscript. The first reading should reveal the primary actions detailed in the playscript, and whether the actor possesses the degree of association and familiarity necessary to select one of the characters for an honest, natural performance in any subsequent audition. This initial reading may also evoke creative ideas for character movement or staging that will give a sense of tempo and vitality to the selected monolog or scene.

A second reading of the playscript — with a particular character now firmly in performance mind — should be more critical and objective than the first reading, and should concentrate on discovering the inherent meaning being conveyed in the words and the actions of the selected character. This analytical second reading should consider the selected character's word choice, point of view, and attitude in the playscript as well as in isolated scenes, and may also include a critical evaluation of the selected character's mood, self-image, or relationship with others in the playscript. The second reading invariably produces character performance ideas that promote active, inventive possibilities for role-playing and for potential vocal or physical approaches to characterization.

Continued reading of the playscript should help to polish the interpretation in terms of expressive character thoughts, emotions, or responses that would give dimension and depth to the audition performance. When combined with critical insight and an imaginative interpretation, frequent re-reading of the entire playscript should provide the stimulating visualization needed for character gestures and movement; provoke theatrically stimulating staging; sharpen the three-dimensional character portrait; define the intellectual, emotional, and physical nature of the character; and suggest initial ideas for suggestive costumes or hand props that enrich stage business. Indeed, it is in the frequent re-reading of the entire playscript that the selected character is more accurately developed and the interpretation more authentically defined.

## BASIC PRINCIPLES

One of the basic principles in selecting promising audition materials should be to establish your age, vocal range, movement potential, and physical type; and you should avoid those audition choices that demand an overly precise use of the voice, foreign accents, exaggerated movement, or highly theatrical posturing or posing. A second basic principle in selecting potential audition materials is to be skeptical of monologs or scenes that do not have a dramatic framework inherent in the selection — three-dimensional character(s), internal or psychological conflict, interesting point of view, and a build to some climactic resolution. Remember that the audition setting is a rather brief two or three minute period of time in the selected playscript, and that you must strive to focus those fleeting moments directly forward to the listening director or staff for the most immediate, memorable impact. In addition, you will need to pay particular attention to the following basic principles when selecting potential audition materials.

- Use a wristwatch with a second hand to time any promising audition monolog or scene before making a final selection. Don't forget to allow time for an introduction to the performance, pauses, and for the audition to build to a climax.

- Use a dictionary to paraphrase the potential monolog or scene into your own conversational words to determine if you can reduce character thoughts, ideas, and actions to one-word nouns or verbs that would be understandable in the audition performance.

- In considering potential monologs or scenes for audition performance learn to isolate and identify significant images and evocative language — what the master acting theorist Stanislavski termed "diction" — that gives character's dialog its expression and meaning.

- In reviewing promising monologs or scenes that have an immediate, personal attraction try to invent a brief character biography that would give added dimension to your interpretation and character portrait.

## AUDITION SOURCES
There are a number of audition sources available to the actor, including anthologies of edited monologs and scenes, film scripts,

personal theatre libraries, annual publication of best play collections, reading lists, and acting textbooks that include recommended monolog or scene materials for specific types of auditions. All of these valuable sources offer a wide range of audition materials appropriate for the beginning actor who may have limited experience in reading a complete playscript with an eye toward adapting or editing long speeches or compact scenes for the audition performance.

As valuable as all of these audition sources are, however, the actor's most important audition resource materials may be original imaginative monologs or scenes adapted from non-dramatic works like poems, short stories, novels, essays, autobiographies, song lyrics, or diary journals. In comparison to the shopworn, familiar monologs or scenes that feature famous or favorite playwrights that now quite figuratively litter the audition stage, original adaptations from less well-known non-dramatic works frequently provide refreshing, innovative materials that more easily reveal the actor's own individual, personal skills and performance techniques. Original adaptations also allow the actor to place a more personal stamp on the audition, and to draw interesting character portraits from contemporary, everyday life.

Novels, as well as short stories and poems, are particularly effective when adapted for the audition performance because of the thread of action that appears to give each its basic unity. Each separate episode, adventure, or story of the primary or secondary character(s) may be easily extracted from the longer text for stage dramatization without sacrificing meaning, form, or character development. The isolation of individual episodes, stanzas, adventures, or stories may be extremely valuable in revealing a selected character's insight or point of view in a given situation, and may also highlight fundamental character traits related to interior psychological states of mind or self-image. If you are interested in adapting or editing non-dramatic literature for an audition performance remember to have a beginning, middle, and end for the adaptation sustain the selected episode with energetic movement toward a climax; include appropriate introductions and transitions that set the scene; promote movement opportunities for creative staging; display the range of your vocal/physical talents; and reveal your*self* in an audition performance that is authentic and honest.

## PERFORMANCE BLUEPRINT

In selecting prospective audition materials the actor should pay special attention to the performance blueprint suggested in the monolog or scene. Of special concern should be the probable ease and freedom of movement, the possibility for vocal variety, and the potential for emotional and intellectual honesty that results in a memorable, stage-worthy audition performance. Remember that the performance blueprint initially suggested in the monolog or scene should provide ample opportunities for the actor to capture an incisive self-portrait of a truly unique character in terms of attitude, gesture, and mannerism. A preliminary review of the performance blueprint suggested in the monolog or scene might also include the following considerations.

- Generates moment-to-moment character interaction and interpersonal relationships with other characters.

- Reveals interesting and inventive stage business to help clarify the apparent subtext of character action and dialog.

- Creates challenging improvisational opportunities that lead to discovery of character intention and motivation.

- Promotes visually explicit movement patterns or pictorial composition that punctuates character, attitude, or mood.

- Encourages a natural, conversational tone of expression that gives additional dimension to character thoughts, ideas, and emotions.

Final selection of audition materials frequently depends upon more personal or practical decision-making as well. The actor needs to feel comfortable and confident in the monolog or scene selected for the audition performance, and that self-satisfaction and self-confidence is a personal measure of following your own instincts and trusting your own judgment. The actor also needs to be aware of practical concerns like the size of the audition stage, the need to memorize the selected monolog or scene, the specific props or set pieces required for the audition performance, and the given circumstances, or situation, described in the prospective audition materials.

Your identification and understanding of the character actions and thoughts expressed in the playscript should lead to a discriminating selection of audition performance monologs or scenes. Always look for appropriate performance materials that promote a character's emotional, intellectual, or physical relationship with other interesting characters, and try to personalize the selected monolog or scene to your own visualization of the character in the situation being described before making any final audition choices. Perhaps that is the suggestion Shakespeare had in mind in his advice to the actors in Hamlet's now famous "Player's" speech:

> To thine own self be true,
> And it must follow as the night the day,
> Thou canst not then be false to any man."
>
> Shakespeare, *Hamlet* (I, iii)

## REHEARSAL BLUEPRINT

The audition rehearsal period is an excellent time for the actor to reevaluate the initial analysis and interpretation of a selected monolog or scene, and to anticipate new performance insights that might surface through experimentation and improvisation. This is a time to be open and flexible in your interpretation — vocal and physical — and to explore the character's inner/outer actions and reactions as well. The rehearsal period is also an opportunity for the actor to fill in the blanks left unanswered in the selected monolog or scene

— especially if there are unresolved questions about character goals, intentions, or motivation. The important point to remember in the rehearsal period is that any reevaluation or subsequent revision of the initial audition performance blueprint must serve to clarify the action, the characters, or the situation. And performance revision should *never* contradict or confuse the basic character information indicated in the complete playscript!

Although the audition rehearsal period is primarily concerned with isolating and identifying a character's mannerisms, gestures, movements, and vocal qualities, it is also a time to discover the distinguishing personal habits of a character that might give added dimension to the audition performance. Some actors use the rehearsal period to search for a metaphor, or implied comparison between the character and something inventive, and to incorporate those imaginative comparisons into the audition performance. Other actors use the rehearsal period to engage in word play with the lines of dialog to heighten the meaning of the spoken words or to punctuate the tempo of the language spoken by the character(s). A few actors use the rehearsal period to visualize the images suggested in the selected monolog or scene and then explore inventive strategies to give these symbols concrete forms of expression in the audition performance.

Regardless of the individual approach you might take to the rehearsal period, there are a number of important principles that should be part of any audition rehearsal. Perhaps the following checklist will give you the initial insight to clearly understand the need for an orderly, well-defined audition rehearsal blueprint that may give meaning and purpose to your subsequent performance.

- The rehearsal period should break down the monolog or scene into a series of character intentions or objectives called beats. A beat begins when a character's intention begins and ends with its completion.

- The rehearsal period should encourage an inner monolog, or what the actor is thinking as the character is speaking. The inner monolog is very similar to subtext, or the hidden meaning or language, and can be used effectively to suggest a character's primary goal or objective in a monolog or scene.

• The rehearsal period should allow the actor sufficient time to complete the research related to the monolog or scene. This might include looking for appropriate books, articles, recordings, films, art pictures, videotapes, or historical materials that help to flesh out a character portrait in terms of potential mannerisms, posture, hand props, wardrobe, or accessories.

• The rehearsal period should permit time to videotape the monolog or scene for a preliminary assessment of vocal and physical performance.

• The rehearsal period should allow the actor ample opportunity to experiment with alternative performance techniques as well. One popular alternative technique is Stanislavski's use of objective memory, in which the actor re-creates the basic stimuli present during a past emotional episode or experience in his/her own life and then reexperiences the stimuli of the past in an interpretation of a similar experience described in the selected monolog or scene.

• Another popular alternative technique is substitution or transfer, in which the actor uses a specific person from his/her own life experience and projects that person's personality onto the character(s) described in the selected monolog or scene.

The rehearsal period is also a good time to begin a regularly scheduled practice session of vocal and physical warm-ups that can later be used to reduce anxiety and nervousness before the audition performance. A rehearsal routine that regularly tunes the voice and the body should establish an exercise program that effectively combats the initial stage fright associated with audition performance. Although you will develop your own personal warm-up exercises as you gain experience and self-confidence, the basic principle in the rehearsal period is to condition your voice and body to respond promptly to any vocal or physical demand, and to discover as many expressive vocal qualities and movement styles as needed to give voice and body to the selected character in the monolog or scene. Remember that it is not enough to rehearse only for the audition performance. Time must always be set aside for introductions, memorization, warm-ups, line interpretation, movement, and characterization if you are serious in your desire to meet the demands and expectations of the audition process.

A final consideration for the rehearsal period is to preview your polished audition performance before an invited audience of personal friends, roommates, family, and fellow actors. The primary objective of the invited preview should be to cultivate a sense of the anticipated reactions or responses of a live audience, and to learn appropriate strategies needed to make performance adjustments without seriously compromising what has been discovered, refined, and then polished in the rehearsal period. The performance awareness that results from audition previews is immeasurable and invaluable to the actor who needs immediate feedback on the clarity and comprehension of the character portrait(s) being drawn. The preview performance also encourages a non-threatening assessment and evaluation of the actor's preliminary decision-making in visualizing character interpretation, vocal/physical qualities, movement, and staging. When you are confident that your character portrait is an accurate, precise, and polished reflection of your playscript interpretation of the selected monolog or scene, stage a theatrical event and have a preview party of invited guests for a gala audition performance!

## PERFORMANCE ETIQUETTE

There are a number of performance etiquette principles associated with selecting audition materials that should be addressed in the rehearsal period. The first principle is the need to maintain at least three copies of the selected audition materials. The first copy should be used to chart appropriate character actions or intentions that are revealed in the dialog, and you should mark in colored pencil the tempo of the actions or intentions to indicate the apparent build to a climax in the selection. The second copy should be used to chart appropriate vocal and physical reactions and responses to words and movement, including the underlining in a different colored pencil operative words or phrases that emphasize potential word play or meaningful gestures that might give dimension to the character portrait. The first two copies of the selected audition materials should be used exclusively throughout the rehearsal period, allowing for adaptations, changes, or revisions to be included as further rehearsal exploration reveals inventive new insights for the audition performance. At the conclusion of the rehearsal period, the final performance blueprint — voice and body — should be clearly marked in the third copy of the selected audition materials, and it is the third copy that should be used to polish the final audition interpretation and performance.

A second performance etiquette principle associated with selecting audition materials that should be addressed in the rehearsal period is the planning of the introduction to the selected materials at the actual audition. It is an expectation that introductions will be brief, set the scene, and feature a description of the main character(s) in the selected monolog or scene. A typical introduction for the audition might be a rather simple and direct, "Hello, I'm Roscoe Tanner. I will be doing the funeral oration of Marc Antony from *Julius Caesar* and the 'rabbit' speech of Lenny in *Of Mice and Men.*"

Following the brief introduction, the actor should move to the center of the playing space nearest the overhead lighting, pause briefly, and then begin the first monolog, pause briefly at the conclusion of the first monolog and then move to another area of the playing space to present the second selection, pause briefly before the second selection, and then present the monolog. At the conclusion of the second selection, pause following the final line of dialog and hold the climactic moment or pose. Then, relax and say a simple "thank-you" to those assembled in the audience before exiting the playing space.

If it is essential to use props or set pieces like a chair or a stool in the audition performance they should be placed in the playing space before the introduction is presented. Remember to set the scene briefly, with no plot summary, personal apologies, or extended elaboration of the character. Don't be surprised, however, if the director interrupts you at any point in the audition performance to ask a question or to request an improvisation or directed reading with suggested character hints or dialog interpretation. Remember, the director may immediately see or hear something in your audition performance that merits further exploration — and you may be under consideration for a role you had not even anticipated!

A third performance etiquette principle associated with selecting audition materials that should be addressed in the rehearsal period is the staging of the selected monolog or scene. The following hints for audition staging are traditional actor approaches that place the performer in the most favorable position to exhibit vocal and physical skills.

- Face the audience full-front, especially in the introduction to the audition material and in the climactic moment of the monolog or scene.

- Place set pieces like a chair or stool down right or down left stage so the center of the playing space is free to frame the actor's movement.

- Locate any imaginary characters being addressed in the monolog or scene in the audience, slightly above the heads of the audience.

- Perform the audition material downstage, and never upstage.

- Limit hand props to those objects which are essential extensions of the character (like Captain Queeg's marbles in *The Caine Mutiny* or Sister Rita's rosary in *The Runner Stumbles*).

- Rehearse in a number of different spaces to anticipate auditions that might be held in classrooms, studios, music halls, community centers, cafeterias, or more traditional theatres.

A conscientious review of performance etiquette associated with the audition process should promote a spirit of spontaneity that will make a noticeable impression on the casting director. Remember that the audition *is* a performance, and the actor must cultivate a rehearsal attitude of discipline that leads to a well-defined and polished audition performance. Being aware of performance etiquette — and anticipating its potential impact on your audition — can be a viable approach to achieving a memorable audition performance.

## ADDITIONAL DIMENSIONS

The additional dimensions of selecting audition materials for performance are related to maintaining a spirit of inventiveness, spontaneity, and risk-taking in the rehearsal period as well as in the public audition performance. As valuable as all of your preliminary preparation may have been for the audition, however, even the most critical analysis and careful attention to detail may not have provided the clues necessary to understand why you may not be cast in a production or reviewed favorably by the director in the call back final selection process. Hopefully, the following additional dimensions will provide those helpful hints needed to give distinction and individuality to your audition performance.

### GOING UP

One of the first concerns of the actor is "going up," or forgetting dialog lines, during the public audition performance. The immediate response, of course, is "Just go on!" If your initial stage fright should manifest itself in this manner, take a deep breath and try to concentrate on the character's next intention or motivation in the monolog or scene. You should be sufficiently prepared through extensive rehearsal periods to paraphrase the missing dialog to cover the demands of the character's spoken lines or to improvise the demands of the given circumstances in the monolog or scene. Remember, you are the only person with a complete copy of your audition material — so if you should happen to "go up," just learn to go on as if any momentary lapses or pauses are an integral part of the audition performance. Of course, you can reduce the possibility of forgetting dialog lines during the public audition performance with appropriate vocal and physical warm-ups that relax and stimulate movement or thought, and with a concentrated, thorough spoken review of the audition monolog or scene before the performance. It is especially important to warm up your vocal cords to extend vocal range before the audition, and to review your dialog aloud rather than silently to focus attention on the immediate character intention or motivation in the selected monolog or scene.

### ACCENTS AND ACCESSORIES

Remember to use audition accents only as appropriate and only if they can be executed with accuracy and authenticity. Try to cultivate a working catalog of performance accents — primarily British, Cockney, German, Italian, New York (Brooklyn), Southern American, Spanish, Oriental, Gypsy, and Midwestern — by purchasing tapes of accents, learning the phonetic approach to voicing accents correctly, or listening to television, radio, or film clips that feature authentic, ethnic accents. It is a good performance idea to practice appropriate audition accents in everyday conversation, whether it is informally with personal friends or more formally in trying to order food or shopping in a mall that features multicultural businesses. It is also a good performance idea to limit accessories in the audition performance. Always wear comfortable, loose clothing that promotes freedom of movement, and select an appropriate audition wardrobe that emphasizes cut or color to help visualize the selected character portrait. Avoid tight jeans, boots, plunging necklines, short skirts, excessive jewelry, sandals, false hair, and glasses in the audience performance unless they are absolutely essential for the character interpretation. Try to suggest discriminating good taste in your audition accessories, and try to refrain from any relaxants like alcohol, cigarettes, caffeine, or pep pills that might actually become negative stimulants that disrupt your audition concentration and focus.

### STAGING AND STYLE

There are several additional dimensions related to the staging and style of audition monologs or scenes, and the rehearsal period is an excellent opportunity to explore the dimensions of each. In staging the audition performance remember to limit set pieces to a single chair or stool, and do not anticipate an elaborate setting or special effects like mood lighting or sound. Your stage blocking, or character movement, should be confined to an isolated space — usually center stage — that focuses audience attention on the selected character's actions and reactions in the selected monolog or scene. Do not litter the stage with distracting hand props or objects that later become part of the audition performance. Neglect of a well-prepared and carefully executed staging blueprint developed in the rehearsal period can result in an audition performance that appears disorganized, lifeless, or static. The style of the audition refers to the spark of energy and vitality that characterizes your stage personality and performance. If you concentrate on the given circumstances, the character objectives, and the intentions being expressed in the selected monolog or scene the energy level of your performance should be at its most effective level of involvement, and the audience should sense your crisp and polished vocal and physical expression of direct and immediate identification with the character portrait being performed. A memorable sense of audition style also involves a more personal, individual characterization that has a unique depth, dimension, integrity, and believability because it is based upon a flesh-and-blood, real-life role model that has immediate audience appeal and addresses significant universal views and values.

### CALLBACKS

A final additional consideration in selecting audition materials for performance is the expectation of a callback for further casting consideration. When callbacks are posted the final audition materials are usually chosen for you, so make sure that you re-read the entire playscript again to review character relationships and potential interpretations. You should also be prepared in callbacks for vocal or physical improvisations, cold readings, and perhaps even an interview session with the director or staff. Try not to plan any responses or reactions in advance, and do not anticipate the character or the scene that you may be asked to perform for callbacks. It is much better to demonstrate spontaneity and an ability to take direction in callbacks than to appear rigid and inflexible in your interpretation and characterization. It may also be a good performance idea to wear the same audition wardrobe to callbacks in order to refresh the director's memory of the initial look that earned you another audition opportunity. Remember to be on time for callbacks, and don't forget to budget time for vocal and physical exercises before your callback appointment. Always be attentive to the callback order of scheduled auditions, and know who you follow in the scheduled order so that last-minute emergencies like a missing button, a drink of water, or a restroom "potty pause" will not distract your concentration on the callback performance.

Callbacks are excellent performance experience for the beginning actor and provide ample opportunities to use one's own personal, unique traits like comic flair, physique, or vocal quality to give an added dimension to the final audition performance. So, clearly define the tidbits of character action and reaction that are indicated in the callback audition instructions, and concentrate on a single callback performance objective and a selective callback character portrait most appropriate to the final audition. This well-focused approach to callbacks should result in a striking performance that has expressive imagination and sensitivity!

## MUSICAL THEATRE

The selection of audition materials for musical theatre is primarily dependent upon discovering interesting characters for vocal performance. The characters of musical theatre usually find themselves in unfortunate, yet comic, situations that afford no convenient means of escape. But they endure hardships and encounter rejection and hostility with the hope and determination that eventually prove their true value. The potentially tragic circumstances that these characters face — losing a job, being down-and-out, dreaming of a better life, or being jilted in a devastating relationship — are invariably resolved through their own ingenuity and integrity, but they exhibit in their strength of character the ability to transcend the immediate consequences of their plight and emerge to achieve a measure of personal distinction. They are at their most exaltated in singing the songs that communicate their frustration and underscore their optimism for the future. By paying careful attention to the songs, the actor should notice that musical theatre characters appear to grow stronger from facing the obstacles they initially see as limiting their potential success. In considering appropriate audition materials for musical theatre, the actor should look for the honesty and frankness in the songs of the characters, and make special note of how the lyrics help to reflect a selected character's basic nature or disposition.

One of the most difficult responsibilities for the musical theatre actor is selecting audition materials that promote a vocal orchestration of the dialog in the *book* and the dynamic sounds of the *libretto*. In preparing for the musical theatre audition, the actor has to make sure that the music is in the correct key for his/her voice, and must take into account personal vocal strengths or weaknesses, extremes of range and style, and interpretations or tempo before making decisions on appropriate monologs or scenes for performance. In addition, the actor has to consider the wide range of musical theatre materials available for auditions like Broadway (*Chicago* or *Phantom of the Opera*), rock (*Tommy* or *Godspell*), operetta (*The Pirates of Penzance* or *Little Mary Sunshine*), musical dramas (*Miss Saigon* or *Showboat*), operas (*Les Miserables* or *The Three Penny Opera*), revues (*Oh, Coward* or *Forbidden Broadway*), and a host of contemporary interactive musicals (*Rent* or *Da Noise/Da Funk*).

But perhaps the most challenging responsibility of all for the actor is a need to demonstrate *each* of the following ingredients of musical theatre in a competitive audition process; and to do so with a considerable degree of skill that results in a "tripe threat" performance of an interesting character interpretation, vocal or physical versatility, and an ensemble singing/dancing talent.

• Be able to learn and execute specialty skills in acrobatics, stage combat, and modern dance, jazz or tap.

• Be able to perform in solo as well as in ensemble numbers.

• Be able to learn and to execute complicated choreographic numbers.

• Be able to express emotion in song rather than in dialog.

• Be able to sustain a rhythmic tune and act song lyrics.

• Be able to sing, dance, and act simultaneously.

• Be able to sight read music.

It is very important, therefore, in selecting musical theatre audition materials to think of potential songs or dances as lyrical extensions of both the character's emotions or thoughts and the dramatic action of the selected monolog or scene. Remember that there is no fourth wall in musical theatre that separates the actor from the audience, and singing and dancing are a shared experience with the audience that helps to propel the musical to its dramatic or comic climax. In addition, musical theatre dialog serves primarily as a vehicle to introduce songs that reveal character attitude and mood in a selected situation, or as a bridge between recitative and reprise voiced in intricate melodies, rhymes or rhythms.

When considering musical theatre material for an audition performance, the actor should explore the inner life of the character. The inner life includes the character's personal philosophy, point of view, and individual personality. Much of this autobiographical information is derived from the character's background or the given circumstances of the musical theatre playscript and should help the actor create a psychological profile from which to fashion an elaborate characterization. The detailed inner life analysis should also enrich the actor's understanding of the character's objectives, which in turn makes character actions, attitudes, and moods more specific in the musical theatre audition performance.

For the song audition it is always a good performance idea to carry your music with you, and to have additional copies available as needed. Although musical theatre auditions usually provide a resident accompanist, serious actors in musical theatre occasionally engage their own rehearsal pianist for auditions. The song audition process — while similar to the traditional theatre audition — also requires that you wait outside the rehearsal room until your name is called to enter. Use this time wisely to review your music, lyrics, and performance blueprint. When you enter the rehearsal room, locate the stage piano and hand a copy of your music to the accompanist before the performance. Introduce yourself briefly, identify the songs to be performed, and indicate the characters in the selected materials as you move center stage. Pause before singing the first song and conclude the first musical selection with a memorable gesture or pose. Identify the second song and indicate the character(s) as you move either stage right or stage left. Pause before singing the second song, and, again, conclude the musical selection with a memorable gesture or pose. A simple "thank-you" then completes the song audition process as you turn to exit the rehearsal room. Do walk slowly, however, in case the director or staff would like to ask you additional questions or extend the audition with line readings or improvisations!

Remember to avoid long character or scene introductions in the song audition, and do not use taped music or a soundtrack in place of an accompanist! It is always better to have a shorter (30 seconds) than a longer audition song to anticipate any possible audition problems. Keep in mind as well that musical theatre stage figures are somewhat larger-than-life, emotions are more intense, and the stage action more focused than in traditional theatre, so select audition songs that allow you to provide interesting, unique character interpretations that reinforce these general performance characteristics.

One of the keys to finding memorable materials for the musical theatre audition is maintaining an active file of songs that enhance your voice. Keep a notebook that catalogs songs in specific numbers appropriate for the musical theatre audition, such as ballads, show tunes, character songs, comic songs, openings or closings, and narratives. The catalog should also include contemporary songs that promote innovative changes in style, tempo, or interpretations to highlight your originality and versatility. It is also a good idea to review trade papers like *Variety*, *Back Stage*, *Billboard*, and *Cashbox* that routinely list the top tunes in a variety of musical categories.

Of course, the more often you audition for musical theatre, the more likely you are to gain self-confidence, maturity, and poise. Look at the audition process as another opportunity to receive constructive evaluation, and use the experience as a learning tool for other auditions that will surely follow. Continue to seek professional assessment from your peers, teachers, and vocal coach, and continue to seek out public performance opportunities that permit an audience to react and respond to your presentation or performance. All of these positive approaches to performance will provide you with a composite portrait of yourself as a performer and prepare you for later auditions that are exciting and memorable!

## SUMMARY

Selecting audition materials for performance involves much more than just the research needed to discover the complexities of the playscript in terms of structure, language, or characterization; it also involves the actor's alertness to events in everyday life or casual observation that may provide the gesture, the attitude, the voice, the mannerism, or the movement that will give distinction and individuality to the selected monolog or scene. That is why it is important for the actor to suit the selected monolog or scene to the type of playscript or the role being cast in the playscript, and to match audition selections with the posted call.

The actor needs to pay particular attention to a comprehensive reading of the selected playscript as well. While the first reading of the selected playscript is appreciative, the second and third readings of the playscript are more critical and invariably produce performance ideas for characterization and interpretation. Continued reading of the playscript provides creative insight and imaginative vocal/physical clues that help to polish the audition performance. Of course, selecting appropriate audition materials also demands an understanding of the basic principles related to establishing your own age, vocal range, movement potential, or physical type, and avoiding monologs or scenes that do not have a dramatic framework.

There are a number of audition sources available for the beginning actor, including anthologies, film scripts, personal reading lists, best play collections, and acting textbooks. The most inventive sources of audition materials, however, are original adaptations from non-dramatic works like poems, short stories, novels, essays, autobiographies, song lyrics, and diary journals. If you are interested in adapting or editing non-dramatic literature for an audition performance, please review the fundamental characteristics needed for the adaptation, and pay special attention to the thread of action that is an essential ingredient in any successful adaptation.

The performance blueprint needed in selecting audition materials should provide ample inspiration for the actor to generate character interaction, invent interesting stage business, and meet challenging improvisational experiments in the rehearsal period. The performance blueprint leaves nothing to random chance and tries to personalize the selected monolog or scene to the actor's own visualization of the character(s) in the situation being described in the playscript. An important principle of the performance blueprint is to chart each character's changing attitudes or moods and then to rehearse in as economical and believable a manner as possible to suggest those subtle changes with a minimum of vocal or physical effort.

It is in the rehearsal period that the actor discovers the distinguishing personal habits of a character that might give added dimension to the audition performance. The rehearsal period is the ideal time to search for a character metaphor, engage in active word play with lines of dialog, visualize selected images suggested in the playscript, and to reduce the selected monolog or scene to beats that may reveal character subtext. The rehearsal period is also the time to begin a regular practice session of vocal and physical warm-ups that reduce performance anxiety and nervousness.

Don't forget to review performance etiquette in selecting audition materials. Of special concern should be the need to maintain multiple copies of selected audition materials, planning a brief introduction for the audition materials, and staging the selected monolog or scene. Being aware of performance etiquette should reduce the amount of uncertainty and frustration that usually accompanies audition performances, and should enrich a well-disciplined, focused approach to the rehearsal period for scene study.

The additional dimensions of selecting audition materials for performance provide helpful hints that the actor will need to know in confronting typical audition problems like "going up," or forgetting the dialog or the introduction, making informed decisions on the use of accents and accessories, incorporating meaningful movement and a personal sense of style into the audition performance, and the expectations of the callback process. Careful review of the additional dimensions of selecting audition materials should arm the actor with sufficient information so that it is possible to anticipate potential problems before they become performance disasters!

There is an extended discussion on selecting audition materials for musical theatre that spells out the need for vocal orchestration and the inner life of the character in the audition performance. Don't forget to review the basic ingredients of musical theatre in the audition process

43

and the special demands that musical theatre performance places on the actor's voice and body. There should also be a review of the general features of the song audition, including use of an accompanist and maintaining an up-to-date file of audition songs such as ballads, show tunes, openings or closings, and narratives.

Remember that you can learn a great deal about musical theatre characterization by using personal observation to build a believable portrait, one that both speaks and sings expressively. Observe people by listening to what they say and by noticing how they express themselves, and notice if their tone of voice is related to their occupation, personality, or status. Listen to their pattern of inflection, rate of speaking, and pitch of voice to discover vocal patterns that might be of value in developing a musical theatre character. Your observation, however, needs to be genuine inquiry, not just idle curiosity. Gather as much information as you can for future performance reference, including age, height, weight, occupation, interest, and attitude.

Having completed your initial preparation and selection of audition materials, it is now time to seek more immediate professional opportunities for public performance that permit an audience to react to your presentation. All of your research, rehearsal, and exercise routine should have provided you with a composite portrait of yourself as a competent and creative actor who is now capable of meeting the demands of any performance situation. And don't hesitate to rely upon your creativity and imagination to provide that theatrical spark that illuminates both the characters and the selected monolog or scene. Now, when the curtain falls on your next opening night, step forward and take a bow for a job well done!

## SELECTED READINGS

The following suggested readings are recommended for the actor who may like to review the basic principles involved in the professional audition process and in alternative approaches to selecting audition materials. The suggested readings may provide practical information related to character building, interpretation, and staging for the audition performance. These selected readings should also provide an imaginative blueprint for a solid audition performance.

Barton, Robert. *Styles for Actors.* Mountain View, California: Mayfield Publishing Company, 1988.

Belt, Lynda. *The Acting Primer.* Boston: Baker's Ltd., 1993.

Berry, Cicely. *The Actor and the Text,* revised edition. New York: Applause Theatre Books, 1995.

Callow, Simon. *Being an Actor.* New York: Grove Press, 1984.

Craig, David. *A Performer Prepares.* New York: Applause Theatre Books, 1995.

Felnagle, Richard. *Beginning Acting: The Illusion of Natural Behavior.* Englewood Cliffs, New Jersey: Prentice-Hall, 1987.

Gardner, Howard. *Frames of Mind.* New York: Basic Books, 1983.

Hornby, Richard. *Script into Performance.* New York: Applause Theatre Books, 1995.

Issacharoff, Michael and Robin Jones. *Performing Texts.* Philadelphia, Pennsylvania: University of Pennsylvania Press, 1988.

McTigue, Mary. *Acting Like a Pro.* Whitehall, Virginia: Betterway Publications, 1992.

Parilla, Catherine. *A Theory for Reading Dramatic Texts.* New York: Praegar Press, 1995.

Stanislavski, Konstantin. *An Actor Prepares.* New York: Theatre Arts, 1936.

Whelan, Jeremy. *Instant Acting.* Boston: Baker's, Ltd., 1995.

Yakim, Moni. *Creating a Character.* New York: Backstage Books, 1990.

# CHAPTER THREE
# PLAYING CLASSICAL MONOLOGS

*"There are gestures that have a language, hands that have a mouth,*
*and fingers that have a voice."*

— Roman Poet

The historical style of classical Greek performance was apparently a reflection of the special demands made upon the actors of ancient Greece during the fourth and fifth centuries B.C. Greek audiences appear to have held actors in high esteem, and it was common practice in the period for specific actors, like Thespis, to attract sizeable audiences for their interpretations of the major tragic heroes in the City Dionysia drama festival held annually to celebrate a bountiful harvest. It was also common practice to loudly ridicule actors whose interpretations were not appreciated. The actor Aeschines, for example, performed so poorly on one occasion that he was actually stoned off the stage!

What emerges from these isolated examples, of course, is that people from all walks of life were devout theatre-goers in ancient Greece and placed a high premium on actors who exhibited exceptional skills in playscript interpretation. But the historical style of classical Greek performance also relied quite heavily upon skills in mine, dance, gesture, and voice. Greek actors had to develop an enormous range of vocal quality to effectively voice the declamatory style of vocal delivery that placed special emphasis upon articulation and enunciation of verse dialog. There was an additional vocal requirement to cultivate a lyrical quality in the voice that would permit the singing of choral odes or recitative written as solo or as duet accompaniment to the character's development.

It also appears that the actor's physical body was an important, expressive tool used to convey the attitude and mood of the character. The classical actor, therefore, was required to have at command a complete and detailed inventory of movement, gesture, and physicalization to reinforce and enrich the character interpretation. The need for an impressive, flexible voice and body is perhaps best seen in the classical tradition of having all female roles played by men, including the great female characters Medea, Antigone, Electra, and Hecuba.

While it is certainly possible for masks, padding, and costumes to transform the classical actor into the image of the female character being portrayed, there is no evidence to suggest that ancient actors were merely "impersonators" of the leading classical heroines. It is more likely, however, that men playing women was artistically truthful for the ancient Greeks, suggesting the universality of the character rather than the gender of the character. It is likely, also, that the classical practice of men playing women's roles promoted a simplicity and a precision in the development of the character to avoid excessive exaggeration and to promote the illusion of truthfulness.

To suggest the basic Greek performance style in playing classical monologs, it is important to understand that honesty and simplicity are the key ingredients in a contemporary interpretation and audition performance. Avoid the temptation to depict the classical style of posturing and posing, or attempts to incorporate historical patterns of stylized movement and gesturing suggested on ancient vase paintings or classical statues. Further, there should be no effort made to chronicle the classical period use of masks, padding, or costumes in the audition performance.

What is important, however, is to approach each classical monolog with sensitivity and objectivity, a relaxed or natural sense of movement, and an animation that suggests concentration and energy. Always be aware of the poetic beauty of the rhythmic lines of the verse dialog, but speak urgently, directly without appearing pretentious or artificial. Tune your vocal instrument to pronounce sounds, syllables, and words crisply, and practice relaxation exercises to free the voice from anxiety and tension.

A careful analysis of the given circumstances of each classical monolog should help you identify and interpret a character's physical actions, and enhance your audition performance ability to indicate who the character is, what the character is doing, where the character is doing it, when the character is doing it, and why the character is doing it. Remember that you are not trying to re-create the historical Greek period in your audition performance, so play the character role with your own voice, body, movement, and inner resources — based upon either lived experience or observation — to suggest a more contemporary interpretation. It is also important to strive to make the actions of the monolog character your own so that they appear to be spontaneous and natural.

Experimenting with movement and pantomime in the rehearsal period may promote well-executed posture or physical reactions that are more clearly defined, and may give your classical monolog performance a here-and-now sense of characterization. The physicalization of a classical monolog character through expressive movement and pantomime may also help you isolate and identify the emotional or intellectual state of mind in the monolog, and give a sense of rhythm and tempo to your more contemporary character development and interpretation.

Remember, finally, that the contemporary audition performance of a classical monolog demands an emphatic identification and response to the character to lend believability to your interpretation. So, direct audience attention to specific classical character thoughts, emotions, or actions with active word play or subtle movement, and make a personal checklist of the properties of vocal sound — pitch, rate, and inflection — that are most appropriate for amplifying your monolog character's voice. This, then, is what gives authenticity to a contemporary audition performance of a classical monolog: The historical character emerges as a real-life stage figure seen and heard by the audience as a well-defined, flesh-and-blood self-portrait.

The classical monologs that follow are freely adapted from the Greek originals to provide a more contemporary approach to an audition performance. In addition to the tragic monologs that are part of the traditional audition performance, a number of non-dramatic monologs from classical literature are provided for your consideration as inventive audition materials. There are also representative monologs from the later Roman period that may be of value in the audition performance. Although each monolog should be approached with an appreciation of the historical period, remember that a truly inspired, contemporary audition performance of a classical monolog is more likely to be natural and simple, with the emphasis upon human nature rather than ancient history.

## *from* **Lysistrata** (Aristophanes)

*Lysistrata has been awaiting the tardy arrival of some Athenian women summoned to the public square before sunrise to discuss a strategy for ending the Peloponnesian War. Her primary concern is to rouse the women's moral indignation or sense of outrage, and to provoke the women to engage in a martial strike that might bring the absent men home.*

**Lysistrata:** Soft, who goes there? By Athene, I could have sworn I heard the women come! O, I must have dreamed it all. That it should come to this: asleep here all night in order to greet my sisters of Greece, who speed to assist me in a most daring plan to end the war which has ravaged our lands for thirty years! O, good morning to you, gentle Athenians! By Apollo, you have risen early to witness this spectacle. But why do you sit there with folded arms and knitted brows, while all around you dear Greece pulses and throbs? O, now I see! 'Tis no small wonder. Most of you be men! By Eros, it is an omen sure. For it is to you we would speak when all have come together here. O, sweet friends, listen to the wise counsel I am about to impart to you. Lend me your ears if you like frank speaking. If you do not like frank speaking, stick your foot in your ear until I am done!

To be blunt, men are like children twice over, and it is far more fitting to soundly chastise them than to beat them, for there is more excuse for their faults! That is why I summon the women of Greece here this very morning. Our leadership is in fumbling hands. They are incompetent and impotent. They press too hard and are now over-extended. They force affairs, come late, and their efforts are piecemeal to say the least. They do not discharge their obligations, will not give an inch, and their tongues are like double-edged swords. And, O, how they love wars! They come grunting and humping home from the hunt, throw a raw piece of meat at you, bark a command or two and then expect the poor wife to sit up and beg like a common cur. O, a plague on the blanket infantry!

## *from* **Antigone** (Sophocles)

*Creon, the King of Thebes, has issued an edict that his nephew Polynices is a traitor and shall not receive the sacred rites of burial following his death in an attempt to overthrow Creon's rule. Antigone, Creon's own niece and the brother of Polynices, refuses to obey the edict because it did not come from the gods, and tries to bury her brother. She is arrested and charged with treason. The ancient prophet Teiresias counsels the angry Creon and warns him of the consequences of his action.*

**Teiresias:** Mark me now, Creon, for I say that you stand on fate's thin edge. You will know when you hear the signs my art has disclosed. For lately, as I took my place in my ancient seat of augury, where all the birds of the air gather about me, I heard strange things. They were screaming with feverish rage, their usual clear notes were a frightful jargon, and I knew they were rending each other murderously with their talons; the whir of their wings told an angry tale.

Straightaway, these things filling me with fear, I kindled fire upon an altar, with due ceremony, and laid a sacrifice among the fire, but moisture came oozing out from the bones and flesh trickled upon the embers, making them smoke and sputter. Then the gall burst and scattered in the air, and the steaming thighs lay bared of the fat that had wrapped them. And I tell you, it is your deeds that have brought a sickness to the state. For the altars of our city and the altars of our hearths have been polluted, one and all, by birds and dogs who have fed on that outraged corpse that was the son of Oedipus. It is for this reason that the gods refuse prayer and sacrifice at our hands, and will not consume the meat offering with flame. Nor does any bird give a clear sign by its shrill cry, for they have tasted the fatness of a slain man's blood.

Think, then, on these things, my son. All men are liable to err, but he shows wisdom and earns blessings who heals the ills his errors caused. Be not too stubborn, too stiff a will is folly. Yield to the dead, I counsel you, and do not stab the fallen. What prowess is it to slay the slain anew? I have sought your welfare; it is for your good I speak. And it should be a pleasant thing to hear a good counselor when he counsels for your own good.

## *from* **Medea** (Euripides)

*Jason, the classical explorer, has abandoned his wife, Medea, in order to make a more profitable marriage with the younger daughter of Creon, ruler of Corinth. Although Medea has been condemned to exile, she is consumed with anger and jealousy as she now contemplates slaying her own children to render Jason alone and desolate in the world.*

**Medea:** O my babes, you have still a city and a home, where far from me and my sad lot you will live your lives, reft of your mother forever, while I must to another land in banishment. Ah, me! A victim of my own self-will. So it was all in vain I reared you. In vain did I suffer, racked with anguish, enduring the cruel pangs of childbirth! Before Heaven, I once had hope, poor me! High hope that you would nurse me in my old age and deck my corpse with loving hands. But now is my sweet fancy dead and gone, for I must lose you both and in bitterness and sorrow drag through life.

Why do you look at me so, my children? Why smile that last sweet smile? What am I to do? My heart gives way when I behold my children's laughing eyes! O, I cannot! Farewell to all of my former schemes. I will take the children from the land. Why should I wound their father by wounding them? No, I will not do it. And yet, can I consent to let those foes of mine escape from punishment, and then incur their mockery? Into the house, children! And whosoever feels he must not be present at my sacrifice must see to it himself! I will not spoil my handiwork!

O, do not do this deed! Let the children go, unhappy one! Spare the babes! Nay, by the fiends of hell's abyss, never will I hand my children over to their foes to mock and flout. Die they must in any case, and since it is so I, the mother who bore them, will give the fatal blow. In any case their doom is fixed and there is no escape. Now, let your mother kiss your hands. O, hands that I love so well! O, lips most dear to me! I cannot bear to look longer upon you, my sorrow wins the day! At last I understand the awful deed I am about to do, but passion now hath triumphed over my sober thoughts.

My friends, I am resolved upon the deed! At once will I slay my children and then leave this land, without delaying long enough to hand them over to some more savage hand to butcher. Needs must they die in any case, and since they must, I will slay the — I, the mother that bore them. O, heart of mine steel thyself. Why do I hesitate to do the awful deed that must be done? Come, take the sword thou wretched hand of mine! Away with cowardice! Give not one more thought to your babes — how dear they are or how you are their mother. This one brief day forget your dear children, and after that lament. Yet they were my darlings still, I am a lady of sorrows!

## *from* Oedipus the King (Sophocles)

*Oedipus, the King of Thebes, has accused his brother-in-law, Creon, of conspiring with the prophet Teiresias to seize the throne of the kingdom. Creon calmly pleads his innocence and responds in anger mingled with self-control as he denies the rash, irrational outbursts of the King's false accusation.*

**Creon:** No, Oedipus, I am neither rebel nor traitor. Not so, if you will reason with yourself as I with you. This, first: would any man to gain no increase of authority choose kingship, with its fears and sleepless nights? Not I. What I desire — what every man desires if he has wisdom — is to take the substance, not the show, of royalty. For now, through you, I have both power and ease. But were I king, I'd be oppressed with cares. While I have ample sovereignty and rule in peace, why should I want the crown? I am not yet so mad as to give up all that which brings me honor and advantage. Now, every man greets me, and I greet him. Those who have need of you make much of me, since I can make or mar them. Why should I surrender this and load myself with that? A man of sense was never yet a rebel or a traitor. I have no taste for that, nor could I force myself to aid another's treachery.

But you can test me if you choose. Go to Delphi and ask if I reported rightly what was said. And further: if you find that I had dealings with that diviner, you may take and kill me. Not with your single vote, but yours and mine. But not on bare suspicion, unsupported. How wrong it is to use a random judgment and think the false man true, the true man false! To spurn a loyal friend, that is no better than to destroy the life to which we cling. This you will learn in time, for Time alone reveals the upright man. A single day yet suffices to unmask the treacherous.

## *from* **Andromache** (Euripides)

*The murderous passion and subsequent remorse of a childless woman who fears that a youthful rival may win the affection of her husband echoes the self-sacrifice of Medea. Here, it is Hermione, driven by fear and passion when deserted by her husband Neoptolemus, who must seek justice and a moral victory. The Nurse serves as the ideal spectator in preparing the audience for Hermione's entrance.*

**Nurse:** O dearest Women, how this day has brought to us
　　　Evil on evil, followed one by one in turn!
　　　My mistress in the house, I mean Hermione,
　　　Bereft of father, and in consciousness as well
　　　Of what she did, to try to kill Andromache
　　　And her small boy, now wishes to die herself,
　　　Fearing her husband, lest in payment for her deeds
　　　She should be sent disgracefully away from home,
　　　Or killed for trying to kill those she should help instead.
　　　She wants to hang herself; the servants find it hard
　　　Preventing her; they snatch the sword from her hand.
　　　So greatly does she grieve, and what she did before
　　　She knows was not done well, and I can hardly keep
　　　My mistress from her suicide, dear friends of mine.
　　　But you go in, go in to the house and set her free
　　　From death, for new friends can persuade more than the old.

**Hermione:** He'll kill me justly. Need I tell you that?
　　　How did you make this error? Some one might inquire.
　　　The visits of evil women it was that ruined me.
　　　They puffed me up with vanity; they said these words:
　　　"Will you endure to have that rotten slave girl here
　　　To share your husband's bed, with you still in the house?
　　　By Hera queen, she wouldn't look upon daylight

One moment in *my* home or wallow in my bed!"
I leant a willing ear to all these Siren songs,
Inflated by my folly and blinded by the troublemakers
For what need had I to keep an eye on him?
I might have borne him children in the course of time,
While hers, unlawful, would have been half-slaves to mine.
But never, never — I shall say it many times —
Should men who have sound sense, who have a wife besides,
Allow the frequent visits coming in and out
Of women; for they teach her only wickedness.
One woman, paid to do it, will corrupt the wife,
Another wants for her the same disgrace she has,
And many from sheer love of sin…and thus the homes
Of men grow sick. Be on your guard against such tricks.
Shut up the house and lock it tight with bolts and bars.
There's nothing healthy in this running in and out
That women do, but many evils do come from it.

## *from* **The Self-Tormentor** (Terence)

*A curiously modern study of the father-son relationship from a classical perspective, the ancient Chremes tries to understand his younger son Clitipho's love intrigues, and to make sense of the nonsense. Clitipho offers a complex explanation of his present dilemma that strikes a familiar note!*

**Clitipho:** Fathers are so unjust! They don't understand young people at all! They think we ought to start being old men the minute we stop being boys. They don't think we ought to be involved at all in the things that come naturally to young fellows. They set up the rules by the way they feel now, not by the way they used to feel when they were our age. Believe me, if ever I have a son, he'll have a father that understands, yes, sir! If he gets into trouble, he'll feel free to tell me about it; he'll know I can forgive and forget. I won't be like my own father — using somebody else to let me know how he feels. Ye gods! When he's had a couple of drinks too many, the tale he tells of what he used to do! But now he says, "Learn a worthwhile lesson from other people's examples!" Ve-e-ery smart! Hah! He has no idea how little I heard of his lecture. I'm about as discouraged as you can be. Look at Clinia, now. He's pretty much fed up with the way things are going, but just the same he has a nice girl; well brought-up, completely respectable, and innocent. That girl of mine is a real dictator, has a terrible tongue, a regular duchess, expensive tastes, and what a reputation! Then when she names her price, I say, "All right!" — because I don't have the nerve to tell her I have no money. I've never been in a mess like this before, and my father still doesn't know anything about it!

## *from* **Agamemnon** (Aeschylus)

*This tragic playscript of revenge revolves around Clytemnestra, who has been unfaithful to her husband and king, Agamemnon. The tragedy opens with a watchman looking for the distant beacon fires that signal the fall of Troy. Later, the captive princess and prophet Cassandra foretells her own death and Agamemnon's at the hands of the vengeful Clytemnestra.*

**Watchman:** The gods it is I ask to release me from this watch
     A year's length now, spending my nights like a dog,
     Watching on my elbow on the roof of the sons of Atreus
     So that I have come to know the assembly of the mighty stars
     Those which bring storm and those which bring summer to men,
     The shining Masters riveted in the sky —
     I know the decline and rising of those stars.
     And now I am waiting for the sign of the beacon,
     The flame of fire that will carry the report from Troy,
     News of her taking. Which task has been assigned to me
     By a woman of sanguine heart but a man's mind.
     Yet when I take my restless rest in the soaking dew,
     My night not visited with dreams —
     For fear stands by me in the place of sleep
     That I cannot firmly close my eyes in sleep —
     Whenever I think to sing or hum to myself
     As an antidote to sleep, then every time I groan
     And fall to weeping for the fortunes of this house
     Where not as before are things well ordered now.

But now may a good chance fall, escape from pain,
The good news visible in the midnight fire.

**Cassandra:** Oh misery, misery! Again comes on me
The terrible labor of true prophecy, dizzying prelude.
Do you see these who sit before the house,
Children, like the shapes of dreams?
Children who seem to have been killed by their kinsfolk,
Filling their hands with meat, flesh of themselves,
Guts and entrails, handfuls of lament —
Clear what they hold — the same their father tasted.
For this I declare someone is plotting vengeance —
A lion? Lion but coward, that lurks in bed,
Good watchdog truly against the lord's return —
My lord, for I must bear the yoke of serfdom.
A daring criminal! Female murders male.
It is Agamemnon's death that you shall witness!
Ah, what a fire it is! It comes upon me.
It is the two-foot lioness who beds
Beside a wolf, the noble lion away,
It is she will kill me! Brewing a poisoned cup
She will mix my punishment while sharpening
The dagger for her husband; to pay back murder
For my being brought here. Destruction!
They call me crazy, like a fortune-teller,
A poor starved beggar-woman — and I bore it!
And now the prophet undoing his prophetess
Has brought me to this final darkness.
Instead of my father's altar the executioner's block
Waits me the victim, red with my hot blood.
I will go in and have the courage to die.
Look, these gates are the gates of Death.
I greet them, and pray that I may meet a
Deft and mortal stroke so that I may close my
Eyes as my blood ebbs in an easy death.

## *from* **Prometheus Bound** (Aeschylus)

*The story of Prometheus — the name means "fore-thought" — is a simple one in classical literature: he stole from heaven the gods' secret of fire and gave it as a gift to mankind. As a consequence of his act of defiance, Prometheus was seized by Zeus and bound in fetters on a rocky mountain to suffer eternally.*

**Prometheus:** Think not that I am silent because of arrogance
Or stubbornness. No, it is thought consumes my mind
When I look upon myself insulted as I am.
Yet who was it but I who, from the first to the last,
Handed out to these new gods of ours their honors?
Enough of that. I should not be telling that story
To you who know it. Listen though to the sufferings
In mortals — how I found them all helpless at first,
And made them able to reflect and use their wits.
I shall tell the story, not from any grudge to men,
But simply to declare the kindness of my gifts.
They, then, at first had eyes, but all their sight was vain;
They had ears, but did not hear. Instead they were like
The shapes we see in dreams, and all through their long life
They mingled all things aimlessly, and never knew of houses,
Brick-built and warm, or the art of wood-work. They lived in
Burrows, like the light and nimble ants down in the deep
Sunless recesses of their caves. Nor had they any certain
Sign by which to know the times of winter, spring with its
Flowers, or fruitful summer. Instead, they acted in every
Manner without intelligence; till I revealed to them the
Rising of the stars and settings hard to judge. And then
I found for them the art of using numbers, that master
Science, and arrangement of letters, and a discursive
Memory. I was first to bring the beasts to serve under
The yoke and saddle; that they might take on themselves
The greatest burdens of mortals. And it was I who brought,
And made them love the rein, horses to chariots, the pride
Of lordly wealth. And no one else but I discovered for the

Sailors sea-wandering vessels with their canvas wings.
These were the arts I, foolish I, devised for men, and for
Myself I have no device of science by which to escape
For the suffering I now feel.

## *from* **Antigone** (Sophocles)

*The classical heroine Antigone acted bravely in refusing to obey the law
of Creon — her uncle and the King of Thebes — and attempting to bury her
brother in a ceremonial ritual. Now, she is led away by Creon's guards to be
walled up and sealed forever against the light of day to die in a vaulted tomb.*

**Antigone:** Tomb, my bridal-chamber, eternal prison in the
caverned rock, when I come to you I shall find mine own; those many
who have perished, who have seen Persephone. Last of all I take that
way, and fare most miserably of all, my days are so few! But I cherish
good hope that my coming will be welcome to my father, and pleasant
to my own mother, and to you, my brother, pleasing too. For each of
you in death I washed with my own hands, and dressed for your graves,
and I poured drink offerings over you.

And you too, Polynices, for you also in death I tended, and for that
I win such recompense as this. Yet the just will say I did rightly in
paying you these honors. Not for my children, if I had been a mother,
nor for my husband, if his dead body were rotting before me, would I
have chosen to suffer like this in violent defiance of the citizens. For the
sake of what law do I say this? If my husband had died, there would
have been another man for me. I could have had a child from another
husband if I had lost my first child. But even with my mother and father
both hidden away in Hades, no other brother could ever have come into
being for me. For it was thus I saw the higher law, but Creon calls me
guilty, brother, and leads me captive on the way to death. No bridal bed,
no bridal song have been mine, no joy of marriage, and no children at
my breast. But thus forlorn and friendless I go living to the grave.

Yet what law of heaven did I offend? Ah, why should I look to the
gods anymore, for I see they do not hear me, but let me suffer the
punishment of the impious for doing a pious deed. If my fate indeed is
pleasing to the gods, when I have suffered my doom no doubt I shall

learn my sin. But if the sin is with my judges, I wish them no measure of evil greater than that they have now measured out to me. Your words call death to hurry for me. O, land of my fathers! O, my city of Thebes! O, ye gods! They hurry me now; they are in haste to have done with me. Behold me, princess of my Thebes, the last of the house of your kings — see what I suffer, and by whom — because I feared to forget the fear of heaven.

## *from* Medea (Euripides)

*Jason, the classical explorer in search of the golden fleece, abandons his wife Medea to make a more practical marriage with the ruler of Corinth's young daughter. Here, Jason offers a stirring defense that he is marrying the Corinthian princess in order to consolidate not only his own political position but also that of Medea and his children.*

**Jason:** Needs must I now, it seems, turn orator, and, like a good helmsman on a ship with close-reefed sails, weather that wearisome tongue of thine. Now, I believe, since thou wilt exaggerate thy favors, that to Cyprus alone of gods or men I owe the safety of my voyage. Thou hast a subtle wit enough, yet were it a hateful thing for me to say the Love-god constrained thee by his resistless shaft to save my life. However, I will not reckon this too nicely; 'twas kindly done, however, thou didst serve me. Yet for my safety hast thou received more than ever thou gavest, as I will show.

First, thou dwellest in Hellas, instead of thy barbarian land, and hast learnt what justice means and how to live by law, not by the dictates of brute force. And all the Hellenes recognize thy cleverness, and thou hast gained a name, whereas, if thou hadst dwelt upon the confines of the earth, no tongue had mentioned thee. Give me no gold within my halls, nor skill to sing a fairer strain than ever Orpheus sang, unless therewith my fame be spread abroad! So much I say to thee about my own toils, for 'twas thou didst challenge me to this retort.

Second, as for the taunts thou urgest against my marriage with the princess, I will prove to thee that I am prudent, chastened in my love, and a powerful friend to thee and to thy sons. Now, hold thy peace. Since I have here withdrawn from Iolcos with many a hopeless trouble at my back, what happier device could I — an exile — frame than marriage with the daughter of the king? 'Tis not because I loathe thee for my wife — the thought that rankles in thy heart. 'Tis not because I am smitten with desire for a new bride, nor yet that I am eager to vie with others in begetting many children, for those we have are quite enough, and I do not complain.

Nay, 'tis that we — and this is the most important — may dwell in comfort, instead of suffering want (for well I know every friend avoids the poor), and that I might rear my sons as doth befit my house. Further, that I might be the father of brothers for the children thou hast borne, and raise these to the same high rank, uniting the family in one — to my lasting bliss. Thou, indeed, hast no need of more children, but me it profits to help my present family by that which is to be.

Have I miscarried here? Not even thou wouldst say so unless a rival's charms rankled in thy bosom. No, but you women have such strange ideas, that you think all is well so long as your married life runs smooth. But if some mischance occur to ruffle your love, all that was good and lovely you reckon as your foes. Yea, men should have begotten children from some other source, no female race existing. Thus would no evil ever have befallen mankind.

## *from* **Alcestis** (Euripides)

*This touching tragedy is about self-sacrifice by an all-too-loving wife — Alcestis — who agrees to die in place of her ailing husband, Admetus. In an interesting departure from the ancient Greek myth, Euripides introduces the character Hercules to rescue Alcestis from Hades and restore her to life. In the first monolog, the Servant mourns the death of Alcestis and describes Hercules, who has attended the funeral in disguise as a drunken guest.*

**Servant:** Many guests from every land, I know, have come to the Palace of Admetus, and I have set food before them, but never one worse than this guest I have welcomed to the hearth. First, though he saw our lord was in mourning, he entered, and dares to pass through the gates. Then, knowing our misfortune, he did not soberly accept what was offered him, and if anything was not served to him he ordered us to bring it. In both hands he took a cup of ivy-wood, and drank the unmixed wine of the dark grape-mother, until he was encompassed and heated with the flame of wine. He crowned his head with myrtle sprays, howling discordant songs. There was he caring nothing for Admetus' misery, and we servants weeping for the Queen. And yet we hid our tear-laden eyes from the guest, for so Admetus commanded.

And now in the Palace I must entertain this stranger, some villainous thief and dog, while she the Queen I mourn has gone from the house unfollowed, unsaluted. She who was a mother to me and all us servants, for she sheltered us from a myriad of troubles by softening her husband's wrath. Am I not right, then, to hate this stranger, who came to us in the midst of sorrow?


**Hercules:** Hey, you! Why so solemn and anxious? A servant should not be sullen with guests, but greet them with a cheerful heart. You see before you a man who is your lord's friend, and you greet him with a gloomy, frowning face because of your zeal about a strange woman's death. *(Drinks.)* Come here, and let me make you a little wiser!

Know the nature of human life? Don't think you do. You couldn't. Listen to me. All mortals must die. Isn't one who knows if he'll be alive tomorrow morning. Who knows where Fortune will lead? Nobody can teach it. Nobody learns it by rules. So, rejoice in what you hear, and learn from me! Drink! Count each day as it comes as Life — and leave the rest to Fortune. Above all, honor the Love Goddess, sweetest of all the gods to mortal men, a kindly goddess! *(Drinks.)* Put all the rest aside. Trust in what I say, if you think I speak truth — as I believe. Get rid of this gloom, rise superior to Fortune. Crown yourself with flowers and drink with me, won't you? I know the regular clink of the wine cup will row you from darkness and gloom to another haven. *(Drinks.)* Mortals should think mortal thoughts. To all solemn and frowning men, life I say is not life, but a disaster.

## *from* Oedipus the King (Sophocles)

*The character of Oedipus is headstrong, self-willed, and arrogant; a man who would be a god. After he discovers the truth of his life — he was destined in classical myth to murder his father and marry his mother — Oedipus blinds himself as he now assumes a more compassionate, human posture.*

**Oedipus:** That which is done was not done for the best.
Seek not to teach me; counsel me no more.
I know not how I could have gone to Hades
And with these eyes have looked upon my father
Or on my mother; such things have I done
To them; death is no worthy punishment.
Or could I look for pleasure in the sight
Of my own children, born as they were born?
Never! No pleasure there, for eyes of mine,
Nor in this city, nor its battlements
Nor sacred images. From these — ah, miserable!
I, the most nobly born of any Theban
Am banned for ever by my own decree
That the defiler should be driven forth;
The man accursed of Heaven and Laius' house.
Was I to find such taint in me, and then
With level eyes to look them in the face?
Nay, more: if for my ears I could have built
Some dam to stay the flood of sound, that I
Might lose both sight and hearing, and seal up
My wretched body — that I would have done.
How good to dwell beyond the reach of pain!

 \*      \*      \*      \*      \*

Where are you, children? Where? O, come to me!
Come, let me clasp you with a brother's arms,
These hands, which helped your father's eyes,
          once more bright,
To look upon you as they see you now —
Your father who, not seeing, nor inquiring,
Gave you for mother her who bore himself.
See you I cannot, but I weep for you,
For the unhappiness that must be yours,
And for the bitter life you must lead.
What gathering of the citizens, what festivals,
Will you have part in? Your high celebrations

Will be to go back home, and sit in tears.
And when the time for marriage comes, what man will stake
Upon the ruin and the shame
That I am to my parents and to you?
Nothing is wanting there; your father slew
His father, married her who gave him birth,
And then, from that same source whence he himself
Had sprung, got you! With these things they will taunt you,
And who will then take you in marriage?
Nobody! But you must waste, unwedded and unfruitful.
O, Creon! Since they have no parent now
But you — for both of us who gave them life
Have perished — suffer them not to be cast out
Homeless and beggars; for they are your kin.
Have pity on them, for they are so young,
So desolate, except for you alone.
Say "Yes," good Creon! Let your hand confirm it.
And now, my children, for my exhortation
You are too young, but you can pray that I
May live henceforward — where I should.
And you more happily than the father who begot you!

## *from* **The Haunted House** (Plautus)

*The role of the sharp-witted, resourceful servant is the comic impulse of the classical Roman comedy. Phaniscus is typical of the boisterous and farcical Roman slave who serves a rather dull-witted, inept master; a slave who is an amusing rascal more often in control than being controlled by his master.*

**Phaniscus:** *(Smugly)* Slaves that stand in awe of a thrashing, even while they're free from fault, they're the ones that are apt to be useful to their masters. For when those that stand in awe of nothing have once earned a thrashing, the course they take is idiotic. They train for racing. But when they're caught they earn and save more welts from whips than they ever could earn and save from tips. Their income grows from almost nothing till they become regular rawhide kings. But personally, my plan is to beware of welts before my back begins to pain me. I feel it desirable to keep a whole skin, as I have hitherto, and avoid drubbings. *(Looks at his pilfering left hand.)* If I only control this article, I'll keep well-roofed; and when it's raining welts on the rest of them, I won't get soaked. For a master's generally what his slaves choose to make him. If they're good, he's good; if they're bad, he gets bad. Now you see we've got a houseful of slaves as bad as bad can be, that blow in all their savings on their backs. When they're called on to fetch their master home, it's: "I'm not going, don't bother me!" I know what your hurry is — itching to be out somewhere! Oh, yes, you mule, now you want to be off to pasture! That's all the thanks I got from them for being dutiful. I left them. Here I am, the only one of the whole gang to see master home. Tomorrow, when he finds it out, he'll give them a morning dose of cattle hide. Oh well, I consider their backs of less consequence than mine. They'll go in for tanning long before I do for roping!

## *from* **Hippolytus** (Euripides)

*The youthful Hippolytus has taken a vow to abstain from physical love and to devote himself to the worship of the chaste goddess Artemis. Aphrodite, the goddess of love, curses Hippolytus and tempts his stepmother, Phaedra, to desire her stepson. Here, the downcast Phaedra voices her new, surprising attraction for Hippolytus.*

**Phaedra:** This is the truth I saw then, and see still;
Nor is there any magic that can stain
That white truth for me, or make me blind again.
Come, I will show thee how my spirit hath moved.
When the first stab came, and I knew I loved,
I cast about how best to face mine ill.
And the first thought that came, was to be still
And hide that sickness. For no trust there is
In man's tongue, that so well admonishes
And counsels and betrays, and waxes fat
With griefs of its own gathering! After that
I would my madness bravely bear, and try
To conquer by mine own heart's purity.
When these two availed me naught, my

Third mind was to die of all that man can say!
I would not have mine honor thus hidden away;
Why should I have my shame before men's eyes
Kept living? And I knew, in deadly wise, that
Shame was the deed and shame the suffering;
And I a woman, too, to face the thing,
Despised of all!

*Later, as Phaedra lies dying she reveals to the Nurse her secret feelings.
The Nurse, in turn, informs Hippolytus, who reacts so violently and with such
disgust that Phaedra leaves a message for her husband, King Tereseus,
suggesting that Hippolytus has violated her. The king then exiles his innocent
son, whose protest is voiced with sincerity and honesty.*

**Hippolytus:** Father, the hot strained fury of thy heart
Is terrible. I have no skill before a crowd to tell
My thoughts. 'Twere best with few, that know me well
Nay, that is natural; tongues that sound but rude
In wise men's ears, speak to the multitude with music.
None the less, since there is come
This stroke upon me, I must not be dumb,
But speak perforce, and there will I begin
Where thou beganst, as though to strip my sin
Naked, and I not speak a word!
    I make a jest of no man; I am truly honest.
No woman's flesh hath ever this body touched.
My life of innocence moves thee not; so be it.
O, had I here some witness in my need,
As I was witness! Could she hear me plead,
Face me and face the sunlight; well I know,
Our deeds would search us out for thee, and
Show who lies! I never touched this woman that
Was thine! No words could win me to it, nor incline
My heart to dream it. May God strike me down now
Nameless and fameless, without home or town;
An outcast and a wanderer of the world. May
My dead bones never rest, but be hurled

From sea to land, from land to angry sea,
If evil is in my heart and false to thee!
If it was some fear that made her cast away
Her life ... I know not. More I must not say.
Right hath she done when in her was no right.
And Right I follow to my own despair!
O, ye walls, will you not speak? Bear witness
If I be so vile, so false! Alas! Would I could
Stand and watch this thing, and see my face,
And weep for the very pity of my life!

## *from* **Philoctetes** (Sophocles)

*This Greek "Robinson Crusoe" drama involves Philoctetes, who has been bitten by a snake and then left to die on a deserted island by his warriors as they depart for the battle of Troy. Years later, the young seaman Neoptolemus returns to the island to persuade Philoctetes that his presence at Troy is essential for a Greek victory.*

**Neoptolemus:** Now, Philoctetes!
Philoctetes, I say! Come out,
And leave that rocky home of yours!
Here, stretch out your hand, and
Take possession of your weapons!
Now that you have your bow, you've
No cause for further anger against me.
But I want one thing from you: Listen.
There are misfortunes sent from above
Which men are forced to bear alone.
God knows my words are true, and you
Must heed and write them in your soul.
The wound you suffered was heaven-sent,
For you angered the goddess Chryse, and
Now you are doomed never to find release
Until you go yourself to the plains of Troy
And see our army doctors. There, you'll be
Cured; and with your bow and me to help you,

You will achieve the fall of Troy. Think what a
Glorious prize, to be the one chosen as the
Bravest of the Greeks; to win, first healing,
And then everlasting fame as the brave
Man who caused the fall of suffering Troy!

**Philoctetes:** O, hateful Time,
    Why do you keep me here alive?
    Why have you not sent me to my grave?
    How can I disregard his words, spoken in
    Good will towards me? Am I to yield now?
    But then, how could I bear to watch my
    Wretched self? Who would speak to me?
    How could these eyes of mine, that have
    Seen all my story, bear to see me surrender
    To my destroyers? It is not the pain of the
    Past that stings me, but what I still would
    Suffer at the hands of my mortal enemies.
    You kill me with your talk, and then leave
    Me to follow my own destiny! O, generous
    Words! How can I escape the lasting blame
    Of the Greeks? What now can I do to help?
    O, voice that I longed to hear! O, vision long
    Delayed! Thy words shall now be obeyed.
    Farewell, my cave and my home. Farewell,
    Meadows, streams, and the deep-voiced
    Roaring of the sea. Now I finally leave you,
    Leave you at last! Grant me a voyage safe
    And sure; to where great Destiny shall lead.
    To God Almighty, who has thus decreed!

## *from* **Antigone** (Sophocles)

*Creon's denial of Polynices' funeral rites — a fate reserved for the worst of criminals — provokes eternal sorrow and tragedy. In the following pathetic description, the Messenger details what has now befallen Creon's son, Haemon, and Antigone in the cold nuptial chamber they now share as spiritual lovers. There is also a soul-searing vision of the heartbroken king as he recoils in horror from the pitiful sight recalled by the Messenger.*

**Messenger:** Neighbors of the house of Cadmus, dwellers within these sacred walls, there is no state of mortal life that I would ever praise or pity; for none is beyond swift change. Fortune raises up and fortune casts down from day to day. And no man can foretell the fate of things established. For Creon was blest in all that I count happiness. He had honor as our savior, power as our king, and pride as the father of princely children. Now all is ended. For when a man is stripped of happiness, I count him not with the living — he is but a breathing corpse. Let a man have riches heaped in his house, and live in royal splendor. Yet, I would not give the shadow of a breath for all if they bring no gladness.

I will tell you what I saw; I will hide nothing of the truth. I would gladly tell you a happier tale, but it would soon be found out false. Truth is the only way. I guided your lord the King to the furthest part of the plain where the body of Polynices, torn by dogs, still lay unpitied. There we prayed to the goddess of the roads and to Pluto, in mercy to restrain their wrath. We washed the dead with holy rites, and all that was left of the mortal man we burned with fresh-plucked branches. And over the ashes at last we raised a mound of his native earth.

That done, we turned our steps toward those fearsome caves where in a cold nuptial chamber, with couch of stone, that maiden had been given as a bride of Death. But from afar off, one of us heard a voice wailing aloud. And as the King drew nearer, the sharp anguish of broken cries came to his ears as well. Then he groaned and said like one in pain, 'Can my sudden fear be true? Am I on the saddest road I ever went? That voice is my son's! Hurry, my servants, to the tomb! And through the gap where the stones have been torn out, look into the cell — and tell me if it is Haemon's voice I hear, or if my wits are tortured by the gods.'

At these words from our stricken master, we went to make that search. And in the dim part of the tomb we saw Antigone hanging by the neck; her scarf of fine linen twisted into a cruel noose. And there, too, we saw Haemon — his arms about her waist. He cried out to us about the loss of his bride, his father's deed, and his ill-starred love. Just then, the King approached and saw him. The King then cried out in a piteous voice: 'Unhappy boy, what a deed have you done, breaking into this tomb! Has grief stolen your reason? Come forth, my son! I pray you — I implore!'

The boy answered no word, but glared at him with fierce eyes and spat in his face. Then he drew his cross-hilted sword. His father turned and fled, and the blow missed its mark. Then that maddened boy, torn between grief and rage, straightaway leaned upon his sword and drove it half its length into his side! And in the little moment before death, he clasped the maiden in his arms and her pale cheek was red where his blood gushed forth. Corpse enfolding corpse they now lie. He has won his bride, poor lad, not here but in the halls of Death. To all of us he has left a terrible witness that man's worst error is to reject good counsel.

## *from* Lysistrata (Aristophanes)

*Lysistrata has assembled the Athenian women in the public square to stage a "sex-strike" in hopes of ending the Peloponnesian War. She is aided in her inventive strategy by the temptress Voluptia, "fair-peach of Athens," who instructs them all in the art of women's warfare!*

**Voluptia:** O, Ladies of Greece! You do me praise to call me forth from my labors to here instruct you in my special crafts. I speak as one who has given much, and often, to her country. I speak as one who knows full well the secrets of formations, desirable positions, size of reinforcements, and all of the military chatter relating to involuntary movements on the part of our enemies. For you, however, I shall be brief! Come, sisters! Pain and suffering are yours. Accept them! You must be zealous and silent and endure!

O, by Pisander! Pardon me, sisters! My passion is such that I forget my purpose. Women of Greece, if you would end the war and secure the peace for which you lie awake each night you must wipe all decency from your face! Steady, sisters! A dose of hellbore to give you a brainwash, that's what you need! And not the common stuff the apothecaries peddle in the marketplace, either, but the special brand from Antigua! Steady, sisters!

Eyes emphasized with kohl and false hair; painted lips and lined brows! Wax and Tarentine wraps and earrings. Snake-winding bracelets, anklets, chains and lockets! Steady, sisters! But no roses! O, by Pluto, no roses! When they lose their fragrance both men and gods stay away; for the odor has a marvelous capacity to drive away all repose!

What you don't possess by Nature you may acquire by imitation, and a little padding! And don't forget that a woman cannot possibly be loved without perfume! So put it here and there and everywhere! And when you walk spring forward with a light step. See, walk as I do and men will gaze at you with wonder; their heads erect and their faces beaming with delight at the sight! And don't forget to let your hands interlace, as though you were praying with each step. And, O, face without chalk! Remember, my dainties, for a woman redness of face is the shining flower of charm. To rouge, my sweets, to rouge! But do not be harsh or frightening; and do not seal your beauty away in scarf or veil! O, sisters, throw off those nets that sore beset you and reveal your loveliness!

There's not a part of you but snares men to their doom! Love beckons in your eyes. Your mouths are songs of grace. Your hands are scions of strength and tiny flowers blossom in your cheeks. If you do not believe my craft, take up the mirror and see how your face has changed! O, receive them with scented hair, in fragrant delicto at the half-moon! O, my sweets, what a noble work of art is Woman! *(Collapses in a frenzy.)* And don't forget to imitate the twelve postures of Cyrone!

## *from* **Prometheus Bound** (Euripides)

*Hermes, a messenger from Zeus, pays a final visit to the bound and fettered Prometheus to see if he has confronted his misfortunes and repented his sins. If Prometheus remains stubborn and unyielding, he will be plunged beneath the earth in an earthquake, and at length be brought back to the light of day, where day after day an eagle will gnaw his continually restored liver.*

**Hermes:** You there, the clever one. The one who sinned against the gods by giving over honor to creatures of the day. You thief of fire! The father orders you to tell of that marriage in which you boast that he will fall from power. And none of this must be said in riddles; tell all of it straight out. It is self-conceit like this that brought you to these sufferings. It seems that you take pride in what is happening to you and will say nothing of what the father wants. You fool! Have the courage to frame your thoughts correctly to your present ills. You are neither soft at all nor melted by my prayers; but, taking the bit between your teeth like a colt not broken in, you try and fight against the rein. If you are not persuaded by my words, consider what a storm and hurricane will fall upon you. Be sure these words of mine are no pretended boasting, but too clearly true. Look closely to yourself, reflect, and do not think self-will can ever be a better thing than good advice. What is this but to listen to a madman's words? This man's prayer is no different than raving. He cannot relax from his frenzy. Well, then, remember what I tell you and do not, when you are chased by destruction, find fault with fortune. Do not ever say that Zeus has thrown you to suffering unforeseen. It is not so. You brought it all on yourself. For with clear knowledge, neither suddenly nor by deception, you will be folded up by your folly in an infinite net of self-destruction. *(Thunder, lightning, and an earthquake)*

## *from* Odi et Amo (Catullus)

*The lyrical character sketches of Catullus, the Roman poet, offer a sensitive and expressive view of practical life. A number of the character sketches are self-portraits, in which the poet reveals himself as both artist and simple man. The following self-portrait sketches a disillusioned man suffering the pangs of despair.*

**Catullus:** If there is any pleasure for a man remembering favors past,
When he feels he has kept all faith and formed no bond
Betraying gods to lie to men: then many years are yours,
Catullus, for this empty and thankless love. For, favors men
May say or do for men have been both said and done by you.

But all was lost in trust to a thankless soul. Why suffer more
Self-torture now? Why not resolve upon retreat from that?
The gods say no. Quit courting grief and look at life anew.
It's hard to drop at once a lasting love; it's hard, but do it.
This is your only hope. You've got to do it, impossible or not.
Dear gods, if you know pity or bring help to souls who feel
The pain of death, look on my pain, and, if my life's been
Clean, take this destructive blight from my soul and sight!
My god, this pain crawls through all my limbs and drains my
Heart of happiness. I don't ask for requited love or for what
Cannot be, her decency. I want to lay aside this foul disease.
Dear gods, restore me through my everlasting faith!

## *from* **Casina** (Plautus)

*The comedies of Plautus are noted for their typically boisterous Roman
flavor of satire, earthy language, and rustic characters who appear to delight
in zany, uproarious antics that poke fun at society and traditional values. Here,
the farm servant Olympio pleads his case of true love to a rival servant from
the city, the more sophisticated and worldly Chalinus.*

**Olympio:** I haven't forgotten my responsibilities, Chalinus. I put
someone in charge of the farm who'll take good care while I'm away. I
came to the city to ask if I could marry that fellow slave of yours, the
cutey beauty Casina; the girl you're so madly in love with. And if I do,
once I take her off to the farm with me, I'll stay put in my headquarters
as still as a hen hatching an egg. The things I'm going to do to you at
my wedding! As sure as I'm alive, I'll make you miserable! What will
I do to you? I'll start off by having you carry the torch for my new
bride. Next, I'll hand you one single jug; and point out eight casks, a
copper basin, and one single path to one single fountain. And if that
basin and those casks aren't full to the brim every minute of the day, I'll
fill that hide of yours full of welts! You'll have such a beautiful crook
in your spine from hauling water we'll be able to use you for a yoke.
Then, once we're out at the farm, if you ask for something to eat, either
you'll chomp hay or you'll eat dirt like the worms — because, if you
don't, I'll have you hungrier than the patron saint of starvation on a fast

day! Last of all, when you're all tired out and famished, I'll see to it you get the rest you deserve during the night. I'll wedge you in the window where you can hear me kiss her and hear her say, *(Switching to a falsetto voice)* "Olympio, my darling, my honey pot, my joy, my life — sweetheart, let me kiss those sweet little eyes! Oh, you're so lovely, let me love you to death; light of my life, dickey-bird, turtledove, bunny-kins!" And, all the time she's talking like this, you — damn you! — will be stuck in the middle of the wall like a rat in its hole! *(Turning away)* And now, to keep you from getting ideas about answering me back, I'm going inside. I'm sick and tired of your talk!

## *from* **Electra** (Sophocles)

*The ancient myth of Electra emphasizes the triumph of retributive justice as a son, Orestes, and a daughter, Electra, avenge the murder of their father by killing their adulterous mother, Clytemnestra, and her lover, Aegisthus; both of whom had conspired to slay Agamemnon, king and father to both Orestes and Electra. In the following monolog Electra plots her revenge.*

**Electra:** I feel some shame if I seem to over-weary you with many tears.
But hard compulsion forces me to do this, therefore bear with me.
I pray thee, think what kind of days I pass beholding her who bore
Me companion with my father's murderer. I bow to them, and at their
Hands receive, or suffer want. Think what kind of days I pass seeing
Aegisthus sitting on my father's throne and my mother, if the name of
Mother I may give to one who sleeps with such a one as he, at his side.
I dare not weep, not even weep, as fain my heart would wish; for she,
That woman, noble but in words, heaps on my head such reproaches.
So does she howl, and he too eggs her on, that spouse of hers, standing
Near; that utter coward, that mere mischief. And I, who await Orestes
Evermore to come and stop these evils, waste away. At such a time,
My friends, there is no room for self-control or measured reverence;
Ills force us into choosing words of ill. Hear, then, what I am purposed
To perform. I alone, with my own hands must do this deed and slay him
Whose hand wrought our father's murder. With all I have I now kneel,
Pray, supplicate. Be Thou the gracious helper of my plan, and show to
All men how the gods bestow their due rewards on all impiety.

## *from* **The Pot of Gold** (Plautus)

*This comic farce of a miserly old man, Euclio, who hordes his treasure of gold in a buried pot provided the inspiration for Molière's later masterpiece* The Miser. *Here, however, the emphasis is upon the mental quirks of the miser and his nervousness over the safety of his pot of gold hidden under the hearth.*

**Euclio:** Now I'll go and see if all my gold is still untouched as I have hid it; for it keeps me racked with utter misery with every moment. I take pains to hide my wealth from all men, lest they know, but they seem to know, in my despite; and all salute me with a greater deference than they have shown me before. They notice me, they stop me, take my hand, inquire about my state of health, my business and what I am about. *(Removes the lid of the pot.)* I'm lost! I'm ruined! I'm slain! Where shall I run? Where not run? Catch him, catch him! Whom, or who? I know naught, see naught, walk with blinded eyes. Know not where I go, nor where I am, or who know I for certain. *(To the audience)* Pray you, lend me your aid. I crave, entreat you, point me out the man who's filched it. *(To one of the spectators)* What say *you*? I'm quite dispos'd to trust you, since you have an honest face. *(To the audience as a whole)* What is it? Why do you laugh? I know you — men who hide themselves with whitened clothes and sit like honest folk. What? None of them has got it? You've been the death of me! But tell me, then, who *is it* has got it? You don't know? Alas! What misery is mine! In utter woe I perish utterly. In sorry guise I go, so much of grief this day has brought; so much of groaning and of misery. Yea, poverty and hunger. None in all the world is more acquainted with grief than I am. For what avails my life, when I have lost so much of gold I'd been at pains to guard? Now others lick their chops at this my loss and my distress — 'Tis more than I can bear! *(Runs about stage, crying and wringing his hands.)*

# Chapter Four
# Playing Shakespeare Monologs

*"Suit the action to the word, the word to the action; with this special
observance, that you o'erstep not the modesty of nature..."*
— *Hamlet* (III, ii)

In playing Shakespeare monologs it is important to recall that the
Elizabethan period of drama made a conscious effort to paint upon a
broad emotional and intellectual canvas; sketching three-dimensional
character portraits of heroic men and women in action; driven by
complex psychological forces that at once compel and corrupt them.
Despite the enormous range of characterization(s) found in the
Elizabethan period, however, Shakespeare alone appears to treat his
creations sympathetically as flesh-and-blood individuals who are
foremost human beings rather than mere shadows of fictitious stage
figures. Typically, these characters arouse heightened emotional
associations or provoke spontaneous physical outbursts that signal an
urge to resolve ancient wounds or to avenge current wrongs.

The historical style of Shakespearean acting is unclear, but there is
ample evidence to suggest that the actors were "presentational": facing
the audience full-front and making little effort to suggest an illusion of
reality. Although the actors may have directed their performance
toward the audience, there is also evidence to suggest that there was
some attempt made to suggest believable character actions as well.
Shakespeare indicates as much when he has the Player King in *Hamlet*
instruct the actors to:

"Speak the speech I pray you, as I pronounc'd it to you,
trippingly on the tongue; but if you mouth it, as many
of our players do, I had as lief the town crier spoke my
lines. Nor do not saw the air too much with your hand,
but use all gently ..." (III, ii)

It is interesting to point out that the typical Shakespearean actor was evidently trained in music, dancing, fencing, and stage combat. Because the playscripts were generally performed in outdoor theatres like The Globe, the actors would have needed to cultivate a resonant, well-projected voice that could be capable of not only being heard in a noisy public playhouse that encouraged active audience participation, but that would also have had to be capable of giving subtle expression and nuance to the poetic dialog spoken by the characters.

The historical actor, then, appears to have been an intelligent, well-rounded performer capable of playing both comic and tragic roles as well as female roles. This ability to effectively portray women in a believable and honest character portrait is also strong testimony to the actor's sensitivity and versatility in expressing the deep emotion and complex motivation of Shakespeare's playscripts. It is important, therefore, for the contemporary actor to approach playing Shakespeare monologs not as historic relics but as current episodes that dramatize a significant moment in the life of a real-life modern character.

As you review the selected Shakespeare monologs, narrative poems, and sonnets that follow, pay particular attention to the words and the suggested actions of each character. Since there are very few suggested stage directions in Shakespeare's dramatic playscripts, the potential success of an audition monolog will depend upon your ability to grasp the inherent performance principles implied in the dialog and then to translate those principles into an imaginative and inventive character portrait. A detailed analysis of the words and the suggested actions of each character should help you understand why a character speaks or responds in a particular manner at a particular moment in time.

The detailed analysis of the words and suggested actions of each character in the selected monolog should also help you understand the subtext of meaning revealed in the dialog, and how to incorporate that apparent hidden meaning into significant character movement and staging. A detailed analysis may also call attention to potential audition performance accessories like subtle costumes or props that may add dimension to the character portrait. For example, your analysis of words and actions may reveal the vocal tone of the dour speech by Jacques in *As You Like It,* the physical appearance of the unnatural and demonic Richard in *Richard III,* the character attitude of the hermit Timon in *Timon of Athens,* or the mental disposition of the dark and melancholy title character in *Hamlet.*

But do not be overly alarmed by the fine speaking that is a crucial element in playing Shakespeare monologs. It *is* important that you interpret and read verse well to give full expression to the beauty and rhythm of individual lines of Shakespearean poetry; but more important is that you voice character lines of dialog with a robust clarity and precision that helps to communicate character attitude and mood. When not written in prose, most of Shakespeare's playscripts are written in "unrhyming verse" that is occasionally punctuated with "end rhyme," or "couplets."

This "blank verse" pattern of dialog is vocally explicit in its own rhythmical pattern of pronunciation: there are five *unstressed* short sounds that are juxtaposed by five *stressed* or long sounds. This alternating pattern of short and long sounds then totals ten beats a line. The stress in emphasis is always placed in the second sound (/) and each line ending concludes in a strong stress regardless of punctuation. The unstressed (X) sounds then serve as a "counterpoint" to the long sounds. A sample of this vocal scheme would include the following chart from Hamlet's well-known soliloquy:

To **be** or **not** to **be, that** is the **ques**tion,"
(X)  /  (X)  /  (X)  /      /  (X) (X)  /  (X)

Although this sample vocal scheme may give the actor's Shakespearean speech a "musicality" of intonation and rhythm, you should avoid any exaggerated vocal gymnastics that appear forced or unnatural. It is a much more appropriate audition performance approach to simply concentrate on speaking Shakespeare's verse aloud with vocal "stress" and "color" carefully orchestrated to highlight or to punctuate specific words, phrases, or images that reveal specific character attitudes and moods. Regardless of the vocal choices you might make for the audition performance, avoid the oratorical, over-precise, sing-song vocal blueprint that some inexperienced actors assume is an historically accurate style of Shakespearean speech.

Remember, also, that personal mannerisms, gestures, or movements in playing Shakespeare monologs should appear fluid, graceful, and natural. Avoid cliché, trite approaches to playing Shakespeare monologs with stiff, stilted movement or highly stylized gestures that attempt to capture the noble, heroic nature of the period characters. Cultivate a posture portrait that is comfortable, concentrating on developing all parts of your body to express a character's changing ideas or emotions. Any movement that you may wish to accompany the audition performance should be carefully chosen to highlight a character's intention or motivation, and you should rely upon economy and simplicity in movement to suggest the life-like character portrait.

The audition rehearsal period for playing Shakespeare monologs should focus on a simple and sincere style of performance that cultivates an alert and energetic use of both voice and body. Remember to balance historical approaches to performance with more contemporary performance styles that are inventive and spontaneous. Playing Shakespeare monologs also demands a heightened vigor and vitality in suggesting bodily actions or gestures that best communicate the character's emotions or thoughts.

Knowing your character's specific goals and objectives in the selected monolog, and the staging that might help to communicate them, will give you an audition performance blueprint frame of mind that is both consistent and convincing. Try to find an expressive, forceful performance verb in each monolog that propels your character immediately into the action and the given circumstances being described. Your careful analysis of the monolog and a perceptive interpretation of the character's attitude, action, and dialog should provide a number of performance verbs to explore in the rehearsal period, and selective use of expressive, forceful performance verbs should also help you communicate character subtext and the inherent meaning of the monolog as well.

Finally, your performance blueprint for playing Shakespeare

monologs should include some creative risk-taking that generates interesting stage business; creates challenging improvisational opportunities; reveals a sensitivity to the action, the character, and the situation being described; and highlights the inner and outer character in terms of vocal and physical characterization. Your performance choices should promote a deeper insight when playing the selected monolog, and should provoke fresh, original theatrical images in the audition performance. And it is playing the Shakespeare monolog with these basic principles in mind that will allow you to experience the personal measure of self-confidence that comes — according to Polonius in *Hamlet* — when you follow your instincts and trust your own inventions:

> To thine own self be true,
> And it must follow as the night the day
> Thou canst not then be false to any man. (I, iii)

## *from* **Henry VIII** (III, ii)

*Cardinal Wolsey, who publicly opposed the marriage of King Henry VIII to Anne Boleyn, is stripped of his authority when it is revealed that he has secretly amassed a large fortune from political intrigue and worldly gain. Here, he bids farewell to his position and power in a speech that laments his sin of pride.*

**Wolsey:** So farewell — to the little good you bear me.
Farewell, a long farewell, to all my greatness!
This is the state of man. Today he puts me forth
The tender leaves of hopes; tomorrow blossoms,
And bears his blushing honors thick upon him;
The third day comes a frost, a killing frost,
And when he thinks, good easy man, full surely
His greatness is a-ripening, nips his root,
And then he falls, as I do. I have ventured,
Like little wanton boys that swim on bladders,
This many summers in a sea of glory,
But far beyond my depth; my high-blown pride
At length broke under me, and now has left me

Weary, and old with service, to the mercy
Of a rude stream that must for ever hide me.
Vain pomp and glory of this world, I hate ye!
I feel my heart new opened. O, how wretched
Is that poor man that hangs on princes' favors!
There is betwixt that smile we would aspire to,
That sweet aspect of princes, and their ruin,
More pangs and fears than wars or women have,
And when he falls, he falls like Lucifer,
Never to hope again.

## *from* **Romeo and Juliet** (II, iii)

*Romeo, the virtuous youth who has fallen madly in love with Juliet, slips away from the masquerade ball and lingers under Juliet's window in the romantic hope of seeing her lovely face should she look out from the balcony above. As the window opens, Juliet appears and there is a lyrical exchange of dialog between the star-crossed young souls.*

**Romeo:** But soft! What light through yonder window breaks?
It is the East, and Juliet is the sun!
Arise, fair sun, and kill the envious moon,
Who is already sick and pale with grief
That thou her maid art far more fair than she.
Be not her maid, since she is envious.
Her vestal livery is but sick and green,
And none but fools do wear it. Cast it off.
It is my lady; O, it is my love!
O, that she knew she were!
She speaks, yet she says nothing. What of that?
Her eye discourses; I will answer it.
I am too bold; 'tis not to me she speaks.
Two of the fairest stars in all the heaven,
Having some business to entreat her eyes
To twinkle in their spheres till they return.
What if her eyes were there, they in her head?
The brightness of her cheek would shame those stars

As daylight doth a lamp; her eyes in heaven
Would through the airy region stream so bright
That birds would sing and think it were not night.
See how she leans her cheek upon her hand!
O, that I were a glove upon that hand,
That I might touch that cheek!

**Juliet:** Thou knowest the mask of night is on my face;
Else would a maiden blush bepaint my cheek
For that which thou hast heard me speak tonight.
Fain would I dwell on form — fain, fain deny
What I have spoke; but farewell compliment!
Dost thou love me? I know thou wilt say, "Ay";
And I will take thy word. Yet, if thou swear'st,
Thou mayst prove false. At lovers' perjuries,
They say Jove laughs. O, gentle Romeo,
If thou dost love, pronounce it faithfully.
Or if thou thinkest I am too quickly won,
I'll frown, and be perverse, and say thee nay,
So thou wilt woo; but else, not for the world.
In truth, fair Montague, I am too fond,
And therefore thou mayst think my behavior light;
But trust me, gentleman, I'll prove more true
Than those that have more cunning to be strange.
I should have been more strange, I must confess,
But that thou overheard'st ere I was ware,
My true-love passion. Therefore pardon me,
And not impute this yielding to light love,
Which the dark night hath so discovered.

## *from* **Twelfth Night** (II, v)

*Malvolio, a puritanical and pretentious house steward to the beautiful Olivia, is a moral hypocrite whose sober pronouncements to others are merely a reflection of his own self-hate. Sir Toby Belch and Maria, comic comrades, devise an ingenious trap to expose the foolish steward when they hide a forged and suggestively worded letter in Olivia's garden and hope that Malvolio will discover it.*

**Malvolio:** *(Sees the letter.)* What employment have we here? *(Taking up the letter)* By my life, this is my lady's hand. These be her very c's, her u's, and her t's and thus make she her great P's. It is, in contempt of question, her hand. *(Reads.)* "To the unknown beloved, this, and my good wishes." Her very phrases! *(Opening the letter)* by your leave, wax — soft, and the impressure here Lucrece, with which she uses to seal — 'tis my lady. To whom should this be?

> "Jove knows I love,
> But who?
> Lips do not move,
> No man must know."

"No man must know," What follows? The numbers altered. "No man must know." If this should be thee, Malvolio?

> "I may command where I adore,
> But silence, like a Lucrece knife,
> With bloodless stroke my heart doth gore.
> M. O. A. I. doth sway my life."

"M. O. A. I. doth sway my life." Nay, but first let me see, let me see, let me see. "I may command where I adore." Why, she may command me. I serve her, she is my lady. Why, this is evident in any formal capacity. There is no obstruction in this. And the end — what should that alphabetical position portend? If I could make that resemble something in me. Softly — "M. O. A. I." "M." Malvolio — "M" — why, that begins my name. "M." But then there is no consonancy in the sequel. That suffers under probation. "A" should follow, but "O" does. And then "I" comes behind. "M. O. A. I." This simulation is not as the former; and yet to crush this a little, it would bow to me, for every one of these letters are in my name. Soft, here follows prose. "If this fall into thy hand, revolve. In my stars I am above thee, but be not afraid of greatness. Some are born great, some achieve greatness, and some have greatness thrust upon them. Thy fates open their hands, let thy blood and spirit embrace them, and to inure thyself to what thou art like to be, cast thy humble slough, and appear fresh. Be opposite with a kinsman, surly with servants. Let thy tongue tang arguments of state; put thyself into the trick of singularity. She thus advises that sighs for thee. Remember who commended thy yellow stockings, and wished to see thee ever cross-gartered. I say remember, go to, thou art made if thou desirest to be so; if not, let me see thee a steward still, the fellow of servants, and not worthy to touch Fortune's fingers. Farewell. She that would alter services with thee, The Fortunate Unhappy."

Daylight and champaign discovers not more! This is open. I will be proud, I will read politic authors, I will baffle Sir Toby, I will wash off gross acquaintance, I will be point-device the very man. I do not now fool myself, to let imagination jade me; for every reason excites to this, that my lady loves me! She did commend my yellow stockings of late, she did praise my leg, being cross-gartered, and in this she manifests herself to my love, and with a kind injunction drives me to these habits of her liking. I thank my stars, I am happy. I will be strange, stout, in yellow stockings, and cross-gartered, even with the swiftness of putting on. Jove and my stars be praised. Here is yet a postscript. "Thou canst not choose but know who I am. If thou entertainest my love, let it appear in thy smiling, thy smiles become thee well. Therefore in my presence still smile, my dear sweet, I prithee." Jove, I thank thee. I will smile, I will do everything that thou will have me.

## *from* **Henry VI, Part I** (I, ii and III, iii)

*The French, in mortal combat with the English, receive unexpected aid and comfort from a young shepherd maid, Joan of Arc, who proclaims herself inspired by visions from heaven to lead the French forces to victory. Here, she wins the love and respect of the Dauphin with her patriotic persuasion.*

**Joan:** Look on thy country; look on fertile France,
 And see the cities and the towns defaced
 By wasting ruin of the cruel foe.
 As looks the mother on her lowly babe
 When death doth close his tender dying eyes,
 See, see the pining malady of France;
 Assigned am I to be the English scourge.
 This night the siege assuredly I'll raise:

Expect Saint Martin's summer, halcyon days,
Since I have entered into these wars.
Glory is like a circle in the water,
Which never ceaseth to enlarge itself,
Till by broad spreading it disperse to nought;
With Henry's death the English circle ends.
Dauphin, I am by birth a shepherd's daughter,
My wit untrained in any kind of art.
Heaven and our Lady gracious hath it pleased
To shine on my contemptible estate; Lo, whilst
I waited on my tender lambs, and when the sun's
Parching heat displayed my cheeks all aglow,
God's mother deigned to appear to me,
And in a vision full of majesty
Willed me to leave my base vocation
And free my country from calamity:
Her aid she promised and assured success;
In complete glory she revealed herself;
And, whereas I was black and swart before,
With those clear rays which she infused on me,
That beauty am I blessed with which you see.
Ask me what questions thou canst possible
And I will answer unpremeditated:
My courage try by combat, if thou darest,
And thou shalt find that I exceed my sex.
Resolve on this, thou shalt be fortunate
If thou receive me for thy warlike mate.

## *from* **The Two Noble Kinsmen** (II, v)

*The nameless Jailer's Daughter has become so infatuated with the young and handsome Palamon, that she schemes to free him from her father's prison. Here, she boasts of her deed but is also filled with the sorrow of a modern teenager who sadly discovers the grief that often accompanies an unlikely romance.*

**Jailer's Daughter:** Let all the dukes and all the devils roar —
He is at liberty! I have ventured for him,

And out I have brought him. To a little wood
A mile hence I have sent him, where a cedar
Higher than all the rest spreads like a plane,
Fast by a brook — and there he shall keep close
Till I provide him files and food, for yet
His iron bracelets are not off. O Love,
What a stout-hearted child thou art! My father
Durst better have endured cold iron than done it.
I love him beyond love and beyond reason
Or wit or safety. I have made him know it —
I care not, I am desperate. If the law
Find me, and then condemn me for it, some wenches,
Some honest-hearted maids, will sing my dirge
And tell to memory my death was noble,
Dying almost a martyr. That way he takes,
I purpose, is my way too. Sure, he cannot
Be so unmanly as to leave me here.
If he do, maids will not so easily
Trust men again. And yet, he has not thanked me
For what I have done — no, not so much as kissed me —
And that, methinks, is not so well. Nor scarcely
Could I persuade him to become a free man,
Here, to this place, in the open air, before
I have got strength of limit. Now, my liege,
Tell me what blessings I have here alive,
That I should fear to die? Therefore proceed.
But yet hear this — mistake me not — no life,
I prize it not a straw; but for mine honor,
Which I would free: if I shall be condemned
Upon surmises, all proofs sleeping else
But what your jealousies awake, I tell you
'Tis rigor, and not law. Your honors all,
I do refer me to the oracle.
Apollo be my judge.

## *from* **As You Like It** (II, vii)

*The world-weary and melancholy Jacques* (Ja'kis) *laments the bitter and cynical view of a world in which human vanity corrupts and destroys. A malcontent rarely given to expressions of pleasure or laughter, Jacques spins a masterful tale of human existence and sardonic vision that captures the essence of man's inevitable, fateful reality.*

**Jacques:** All the world's a stage,
    And all the men and women merely players.
    They have their exits and their entrances,
    And one man in his time plays many parts,
    His acts being seven ages. At first the infant,
    Mewling and puking in the nurse's arms.
    Then the whining schoolboy with his satchel
    And shining morning face, creeping like snail
    Unwillingly to school. And then the lover,
    Sighing like furnace, with a woeful ballad,
    Made to his mistress' eyebrow. Then, a soldier,
    Full of strange oaths, and bearded like the pard,
    Jealous in honor, sudden, and quick in quarrel,
    Seeking the bubble reputation even in the cannon's
    Mouth. And then the justice, in fair round belly
    With good capon lined, with eyes severe and beard
    Of formal cut, full of wise saws and modern instances;
    And so he plays his part. The sixth age shifts into the
    Lean and slippered pantaloon, with spectacles on nose
    And pouch on side, his youthful hose, well saved, a
    World too wide for his shrunk shank, and his big, manly
    Voice, turning again toward childish treble, pipes and
    Whistles in his sound. Last scene of all, that ends this
    Strange, eventful history, is second childishness
        and mere
    Oblivion, sans teeth, sans eyes, sans taste, sans
        everything.

# *from* **Henry VI, Part III** (III, iv)

*On a rugged battlefield near the outskirts of Wakefield, "Captain Margaret," stern and fierce Queen of England, leads her troops in the capture of Richard, Duke of York; an ambitious nobleman who is trying to seize King Henry's crown. Queen Margaret here displays a cruel and mocking tone as she drags a terrified York to a molehill for his "mock coronation."*

**Queen Margaret:** Hold, Clifford and Northumberland,
Come make him stand upon this molehill here,
That wrought at mountains with outstretched arms
Yet parted but the shadow with his hand.
What — was it you that would be England's king?
Was't you that revelled in our Parliament,
And made a preachment of your high descent?
Where are your mess of sons to back you now?
The wanton Edward and the lusty George?
And where's that valiant crookback prodigy,
Dickie, your boy, that with his grumbling voice
Was wont to cheer his dad in mutinies?
Or with the rest where is your darling Rutland?
Look, York, I stained this napkin with the blood
That valiant Clifford with his rapier's point
Made issue from the bosom of thy boy.
And if thine eyes can water for his death,
I give thee this to dry thy cheeks withal.
Alas, poor York, but that I hate thee deadly
I should lament thy miserable state.
I prithee, grieve, to make me merry, York.
What — hath thy fiery heart so parched thine
Entrails that not a tear can fall for Rutland's death?
Why art thou patient, man? Thou shouldst be mad,
And I, to make thee mad, do mock thee thus.
Stamp, rave, and fret, that I may sing and dance.
Thou wouldst be fee'd, I see, to make me sport.
York cannot speak unless he wear a crown.
A crown for York, and, lords, bow low to him.

Hold you his hands whilst I do set it on.
*(Places paper crown on York's head.)*
Ay, marry, sir, now looks he like a king,
Ay, this is he that took King Henry's chair,
And this is he was his adopted heir.
But how is it that great Plantagenet
Is crowned so soon and broke his solemn oath?
As I bethink me, you should not be king
Till our King Henry had shook hands with death.
And will you pale your head in Henry's glory,
And rob his temples of the diadem
Now, in his life, against your holy oath?
O, 'tis a fault too, too, unpardonable.
Off with the crown,
*(She knocks the crown from his head.)*
And with the crown his head!
And whilst we breathe, take time to do him dead.

## *from* **Macbeth** (II, ii)

*As a comic counterpoint to Macbeth's murder of King Duncan, a drunken Porter at the gates of the castle offers a satiric perspective on the chaos that has broken loose inside the castle. The Porter's stupor, in which he imagines that he is the gatekeeper of Hell, only adds to the noisy farce and sardonic humor that gives this cameo monolog its intensity.*

**Porter:** Here's a knocking indeed! If a man were porter of
hell-gate he should have old turning the key.
*(Knock within)*
Knock, knock, knock. Who's there, i' th' name of
Beelzebub? Here's a farmer that hanged himself
on th' expectation of plenty. Come in time! Have
napkins enough about you; here you'll sweat for't
*(Knock within)*
Knock, knock. Who's there, in the other devil's
name? Faith, here's an equivocator that could
swear in both the scales against either scale, who

committed treason enough for God's sake, yet
could not equivocate to heaven. O, come in, equivocator.
*(Knock within)*
Knock, knock, knock. Who's there? 'Faith, here's
an English tailor come hither for stealing out of a
French hose. Come in, tailor. Here you may roast your
goose.
*(Knock within)*
Knock, knock. Never at quiet. What are you —?
But this place is too cold for hell. I'll devil-porter it
no further. I had thought to have let in some of all
professions that go the primrose way to th' everlasting
bonfire.
*(Knock within)*
Anon, anon!
*(He opens the gate.)*
I pray you, remember the porter!

## *from* **As You Like It** (III, iv)

*In the magical forest of Arden, Rosalind — an attractive young maiden
wounded by the sad arrows of a failed love affair — innocently stumbles upon
the saucy shepherdess Phebe. Now disguised as the dashing male Ganymede,
Rosalind rebukes the fumbling advances of the unsuspecting country bumpkin
Phebe. But the lovesick Phebe becomes infatuated with the handsome
Ganymede and offers the following tender confession to her companion Silvius.*

**Phebe:** Think not I love him, though I ask for him.
    'Tis but a peevish boy. Yet he talks well.
    But what care I for words? Yet words do well
    When he that speaks them pleases those that hear.
    It is a pretty youth — not very pretty —
    But sure he's proud; and yet his pride becomes him.
    He'll make a proper man. The best thing in him
    Is his complexion; and faster than his tongue
    Did make offence, his eye did heal it up.
    He is not very tall; yet for all his years he's tall.

His leg is but so-so; and yet 'tis well.
There was a pretty redness in his lip,
A little riper and more lusty-red
Than that mixed in his cheek. There be
Some women, Silvius, had they marked him
In parcels as I did, would have gone near
To fall in love with him; but for my part,
I love him not, nor hate him not. And yet
Have I more cause to hate him than to love him.
For what had he to do to chide at me?
He said mine eyes were black, and my hair black;
And now I remembered, scorned at me.
I marvel why I answered not again.
But that's all one. Omittance is no quittance.
I'll write to him a very taunting letter,
And thou shalt bear it. Wilt thou, Silvius?

*In the Epilogue concluding this comic romp, Rosalind addresses the audience to offer one last theatrical laugh. There is a gentle sweetness in her call to the men and women assembled to embrace the mystery of her previous Ganymede disguise and to bid her farewell now that all understand the proper conduct of true lovers.*

**Rosalind:** It is not the fashion to see the lady in the Epilogue.
But it is no more unhandsome than to see the lord in the Prologue.
If it be true that good wine needs no bush, 'tis true that a good play
Needs no epilogue. Yet to good wine they do use good bushes,
And good plays prove the better by the help of good Epilogues.
What a case am I in then, that am neither a good epilogue
Nor cannot insinuate with you in the behalf of a good play!
I am not furnished like a beggar, therefore to beg will not
Become me. My way is to conjure you; and I'll begin with the
Women. I charge you, O women, for the love you bear to women —
As I perceive by your simpering none of you hates me — that
Between you and the women the play may please. If I were a
Woman I would kiss as many of you as had beards that pleased
Me, complexion that liked me, and breaths that I defied not. And

I am sure, as many as have good beards, or good faces, or sweet
Breaths will for my kind offer, when I make curtsy, bid me farewell!

## *from* **Cymbeline** (II, iii)

*Pisanio — a virtuous friend of Posthumus — has been commanded to
murder Imogen, the fair and virtuous wife of Posthumus suspected of adultery.
But the trusted messenger becomes convinced that Imogen is the victim of
some villainous plot to rob her of her honest virtue and hesitates to execute his
friend's command. Here, Imogen pleads her innocence and reaffirms the
sanctity of her marriage vows that remain unbroken.*

**Imogen:** Pisanio, what is in thy mind that makes thee stare thus?
Wherefore breaks that sign, from th' inward of thee? *(Reads note.)*
False to his bed? What is it to be false? To lie in watch there,
And to think on him? To weep 'twixt clock and clock?
If sleep charge nature, to break it with a fearful dream of him
And cry myself awake? That's false to his bed, is it?
I false? Thy conscience witness! Poor I am stale, a
Garment out of fashion, and, for I am richer than to hang
By th' walls, I must be ripped. To pieces with me!
*(Takes his sword.)*
O, men's vows are women's traitors! All good seeming,
By thy revolt, O husband, shall be thought put on for
Villainy, not born where it grows, but worn a bait for me.
Come, fellow, be thou honest; do thou thy master's
Bidding. When thou seest him, a little witness my
Obedience. Look, I draw the sword myself. Take it,
And hit the innocent mansion of my love, my heart!
Fear not, 'tis empty of all things but grief. Thy master
Is not there, who was indeed the riches of it. Do his
Bidding, strike! Thou mayst be valiant in a better cause,
But now thou seem'st a coward!

## *from* **Richard III** (I, i)

*The unnatural and demonic Richard is frequently thought of as the Prince of Darkness, a murderous stage figure who delights in vice and violence. But he is also an accomplished actor, a master with language who is unabashedly theatrical. In the opening of the playscript he beckons us at once into the center of his thoughts and reveals his plan of action.*

**Richard:** Now is the winter of our discontent
Made glorious summer by this son of York;
And all the clouds that loured upon our house
In the deep bosom of the ocean buried.
Now are our brows bound with victorious wreaths,
Our bruised arms hung up for monuments,
Our stem alarums changed to merry meetings,
Our dreadful marches to delightful measures.
Grim-visaged war hath smoothed his wrinkled front,
And now — instead of mounting barbed steeds
To fright the souls of fearful adversaries —
He capers nimbly in a lady's bedchamber
To the lascivious pleasing of a lute.
But I, that am not shaped for sportive tricks
Nor made to court an amorous looking glass;
I, that am rudely stamped, and want love's majesty
To strut before a wanton ambling nymph;
I, that am curtailed to this fair proportion,
Cheated of feature by dissembling Nature,
Deformed, unfinished, sent before my time
Into this breathing world scarce half made up —
And that so lamely and unfashionable
That dogs bark at me as I halt by them —
Why, I, in this weak piping time of peace
Have no delight to pass away the time,
Unless to spy my shadow on the sun
And descant on my own deformity.
And therefore, since I cannot prove a lover
To entertain these fair well-spoken days,

I am determined to prove a villain
And hate the idle pleasures of these days.
Plots have I laid, inductions dangerous,
By drunken prophecies, libels and dreams,
To set my brother Clarence and the King
In deadly hate the one against the other.
And if King Edward be as true and just
As I am subtle, false, and treacherous,
This day should Clarence closely be mewed up
About a prophecy that says that "G"
Of Edward's heirs the murderer shall be.

## *from* **All's Well That Ends Well** (I, i)

*Helena, a virtuous and highly principled woman, is very disturbed about what she perceives to be a lack of moral value in society; and is particularly distressed to observe that chastity is no longer admired as a virtue. She asks Parolles, a wanton braggart, why men appear to be such enemies of virginity, and how virtuous women may guard against an assault on their reputation. Here is Parolles' clinical and matter-of-fact response.*

**Parolles:** It is not politic in the commonwealth of nature to preserve virginity. Loss of virginity is rational increase, and there was never virgin got till virginity was first lost. That you were made of is mettle to make virgins. Virginity, by being once lost, may be ten times found; by being ever kept, it is ever lost. 'Tis too cold a companion; away with it! There's little can be said in't. 'Tis against the rule of nature. To speak on the part of virginity is to accuse your mothers, which is most infallible disobedience. He that hangs himself is a virgin: virginity murders itself, and should be buried in highways, out of all sanctified limit, as a desperate offendress against nature. Virginity breeds mites, much like cheese; consumes itself to the very paring, and so dies with feeding his own stomach. Besides, virginity is peevish, proud, idle, made of self-love — which is the most inhibited sin in the canon. Keep it not, you cannot choose but lose by it. Out with't! Within one year it will make itself two, which is a goodly increase; and the principal itself not much the worse. Away with it! 'Tis a commodity will lose the gloss with lying: the longer kept, the less worth. Off with't while 'tis vendible. Answer the time of request. Virginity, like an old courtier, wears her cap out of fashion, richly suited but unsuitable, just like the brooch and the toothpick, which wear not now. Your date is better in your pie and your porridge than in your cheek, and your virginity, your old virginity, is like one of our French withered pears: it looks ill, it eats drily, marry, 'tis a withered pear — it was formerly better, marry, yet 'tis a withered pear. Have nothing to do with it!

## *from* **Antony and Cleopatra** (II, ii)

*The soldier Enobarbus, friend and confidant of Antony, gives an almost cinematic and erotic description of Queen Cleopatra, the Egyptian temptress. In recalling his first impressions of Queen Cleopatra to male dinner companions back in Rome, Enobarbus's recollection is more of an elaborate hymn of seductive fascination and praise than a simple retelling of the events he witnessed while in Egypt.*

**Enobarbus:** The barge she sat in, like a burnished throne
    Burned on the water. The ship was beaten gold;
    Purple the sails, and so perfumed that the winds
    Were lovesick with them. The oars were silver,
    Which to the tune of flutes kept stroke, and made
    The water which they beat to follow faster,
    As amorous of their strokes. For her own person,
    It beggared all description. She did lie in her
    Pavilion — cloth of gold, of tissue — o'er picturing
    That Venus where we see the fancy outwork nature.
    On each side her stood pretty dimpled boys, like
    Smiling Cupids, with divers-colored fans whose
    Wind did seem to glow the delicate cheeks which
    They did cool, and what they undid did. I saw her
    Once hop forty paces through the public street,
    And having lost her breath, she spoke and panted,
    That she did make defect perfection, and breathless,
    Pour breath from. Age cannot wither her, nor custom
    State her infinite variety. Other women cloy the appetites

They feed, but she makes hungry where most she
Satisfies. For vilest things become themselves in her,
That the holy priests bless her when she is riggish.

## *from* **Hamlet** (II, ii)

*Having welcomed a travelling troupe of players to the castle for a command performance, Hamlet watches a rehearsal in progress and then resolves to act out his own role as an avenger for his father's murder. Here, Hamlet compares the player's passion in playing a fictional stage character to the real-life role he must now assume and act out with the same passion.*

**Hamlet:**                Now I am alone.
O, what a rogue and peasant slave am I!
Is it not monstrous that this player here,
But in a fiction, in a dream of passion,
Could force his soul so to his own conceit
That from her working all his visage wanned,
Tears in his eyes, distraction in his aspect,
A broken voice, and his whole function suiting
With forms to his conceit? And all for nothing.
He would drown the stage with tears, and
Cleave the general ear with horrid speech,
Make mad the guilty and appall the free,
Confound the ignorant, and amaze indeed
The very faculty and eyes and ears.

        \*     \*     \*     \*

                Am I a coward?
Who calls me villain, breaks my pate across,
Plucks off my beard and blows it in my face,
Tweaks me by th' nose, gives me the lie i' th' throat
As deep as to the lungs? Who does this to me?
Ha? 'Swounds, I should take it; for it cannot be
But I am pigeon-livered and lack the gall for action.
Bloody, bawdy villain! Remorseless, treacherous,
Lecherous, kindless villain! O, vengeance! —

Why, what an ass am I? Ay, sure this is most brave,
That I, the son of a dear father murdered, prompted to
My revenge by heaven and hell, must, like a whore,
Unpack my heart with words and fall a-cursing like a
Very drab, a scullion! Fie upon't! About, my brain!
I have heard that guilty creatures sitting at a play
Have by the very cunning of the scene,
Been struck so to the soul that presently
They have proclaimed their malefactions;
For murder, though it have no tongue, will speak
With most miraculous organ. I'll have these players
Play something like the murder of my beloved father
Before mine uncle. I'll observe his looks and then
I'll tent him to the quick. If he but blench, I know my
Course. The spirit that I have seen may be the devil,
And the devil hath power to assume a pleasing shape;
Yea, and perhaps, out of my weakness and my
          melancholy —
As he is very potent with such spirits — abuses me to
          damn me
I'll have grounds more relative than this.
          The play's the thing
Wherein I'll catch the conscience of the King!

## *from* **Timon of Athens** (IV, i)

*Surrounded by fair-weather flatterers, Timon of Athens is a wealthy nobleman and generous friend who is noted for his unbridled extravagance. One by one, however, Timon's friends soon desert him and his creditors send agents to collect outstanding loans. In despair, Timon resolves to exile himself in a cave outside of Athens. There, while digging for roots to gnaw, he voices his bitter curses against mankind.*

**Timon:** *(Digs.)* Nature, being sick of man's unkindness,
          Should yet be hungry! Common mother, thou
          Whose womb unmeasurable and infinite breast

Teems and feeds all; those selfsame mettle
Whereof thy proud child, arrogant man, is puffed
Engenders the black toad and adder blue,
The gilded newt and the eyeless venomed worm,
With all th' abhorred births, below crisp heaven
Whereon Hyperion's quick'ning fire doth shine —
Yield him who all thy human sons doth hate,
From forth thy plenteous bosom, one poor root!
Ensear thy fertile and conceptious womb;
Let it no more bring out ingrateful man!
Go great with tigers, wolves, and bears;
Teem with new monsters whom thy upward face
Hath to the marbled mansion all above
Never presented! O, a root! Dear thanks!
Dry up thy marrows, vines, and plough-torn leas,
Whereof ingrateful man with liquorish drafts
And morsels unctuous greases his pure mind,
That from it all consideration slips. Plague!
I am sick of this false world, and will love naught
But even the mere necessities upon't.
Then, Timon, presently prepare thy grave.
Lie where the light foam of the sea may beat
Thy gravestone daily. Make thine epitaph,
That death in me at others' lives may laugh!

## *from* **King John** (III, iv)

*The French King Philip and Cardinal Pandulph are trying to comfort Lady Constance as she laments for her dead son, Arthur. There is no question about the degree of her passion, but Constance appears so distracted in her grief that the observers question her sanity; and fear she may do harm to herself.*

**Constance:** No, I defy all counsel, all redress,
But that which ends all counsel, true redress —
Death! Death! O amiable, lovely death!
Thou odiferous stench! Sound rottenness!
Come, grin on me, and I will think thou smilest

And buss thee as thy wife. Misery's love,
O, come to me! Thou are not holy to belie me so!
I am not mad. This hair I tear is mine.
My name is Constance. I was Geoffrey's wife.
Young Arthur is my son, and he is lost!
I am not mad — I would to heaven I were,
For then 'tis like I should forget myself!
O, if I could, what grief should I forget!
Preach some philosophy to make me mad,
And thou shalt be canonized, Cardinal!
Grief fills the room up of my absent child,
Lies in his bed, walks up and down with me,
Puts on his pretty looks, repeats his words,
Remembers me of all his gracious parts,
Stuffs out his vacant garments with his form;
Then have I reason to be fond of grief?
Fare you well. Had you such a loss as I,
I could give better comfort than you do.
O Lord! My boy, my Arthur, my fair son!
My life, my joy, my food, my all the world!
My widow-comfort, and my sorrow's cure!

## *from* The Sonnets

*Shakespeare's sonnets can be excellent audition performance material because they are rich in characterization, compact and complete in themselves, and very similar to a self-contained monolog. The sample sonnets that follow are a direct address to either a handsome young man or a dark lady who is wanton. Shakespeare appears to have loved both and they apparently betrayed him with one another.*

## 29

When, in disgrace with Fortune and men's eyes,
I all alone beweep my outcast state,
And trouble deaf heaven with my bootless cries,
And look upon myself and curse my fate —
Wishing me like to one more rich in hope,
Featur'd like him, like him with friends possess'd,
Desiring this man's art, and that man's scope,
With what I most enjoy contented least;
Yet in these thoughts myself almost despising
Haply I think on thee, and then my state,
Like to the lark at break of day arising
From sullen earth, sings hymns at heaven's gate:
   For thy sweet love remember'd such wealth brings
   That then I scorn to change my state with kings.

## 116

Let me not to the marriage of true minds
Admit impediments: love is not love
Which alters when it alteration finds,
Or bends with the remover to remove.
Oh no! It is an ever-fixed mark
That looks on tempests and is never shaken;
It is the star to every wandering bark,
Whose worth's unknown although his height be taken.
Love's not Time's fool, though rosy lips and cheeks
Within his bending sickle's compass come;
Love alters not with his brief hours and weeks,
But bears it out even to the edge of doom.
   If this be error and upon me prov'd,
   I never writ, nor no man ever lov'd.

## *from* **Julius Caesar** (II, i)

*The rational, intellectual Brutus meets his fellow conspirators to contemplate the murder of Caesar. Although alarmed and fearful of Caesar's growing ambition, Brutus is as volatile as he is variable in his commitment to the murder plot. He expresses his initial unease and subsequent resolution in the following exchange with the conspirators.*

**Brutus:** No, not an oath. If not the face of men
   The sufferance of our souls, the time's abuse —
   If these be motives weak, break off betimes,
   And every man hence to his idle bed;
   So let high-sighted tyranny range on
   Till each man drop by lottery. But if these,
   As I am sure they do, bear fire enough
   To kindle cowards and to steel with valour
   The melting spirits of women, then, countrymen,
   What need we any spur but our own cause
   To prick us to redress?…but do not stain
   The even virtue of our enterprise,
   Nor th'insuppressive mettle of our spirits,
   To think that or our cause of performance
   Did need an oath; when every drop of blood
   That every Roman bears, and nobly bears,
   Is guilty of a several bastardy,
   If he do break the smallest particle
   Of any promise that hath passed from him.

       \*     \*     \*     \*

   Our course will seem too bloody, Caius Cassius,
   To cut the head off and then hack the limbs,
   Like wrath in death and envy afterwards;
   For Antony is but a limb of Caesar.
   Let us be sacrificers, but not butchers, Caius,
   We all stand up against the spirit of Caesar,
   And in the spirit of men there is no blood.

O, that we then could come by Caesar's spirit,
And not dismember Caesar! But, alas,
Caesar must not bleed for it. And, gentle friends,
Let's kill him boldly, but not wrathfully;
Let's carve him as a dish fit for the gods,
Not hew him as a carcass for the hounds.

## *from* **Henry IV, Part II** (II, i)

*Mistress Quickly, the saucy hostess-owner of the Boar's Head Tavern, is in a foul mood and desires to have Sir John Falstaff, her carefree vagabond and roustabout companion, arrested for failing to pay his huge eating and drinking debt. On a London street, she happens to meet the unsuspecting Falstaff and vents her anger in the following humorous tirade.*

**Mistress Quickly:** Marry, if thou wert an honest man, thyself, and the money too! Thou didst swear to me upon a parcel-gilt goblet, sitting in my Dolphin chamber, at the round table, by a sea-coal fire, upon Wednesday in Wheeson week, when the Prince broke thy head for liking his father to a singing-man of Windsor — thou didst swear to me then, as I was washing thy wound, to marry me, and make me my lady thy wife. Canst thou deny it! Did not goodwife Keech the butcher's wife come in then, and call me "Gossip Quickly" — coming in to borrow a mess of vinegar, telling us she had a good dish of prawns, whereby thou didst desire to eat some, whereby I told thee they were ill for a green wound? And didst thou not, when she was gone downstairs, desire me to be no more so familiar with such poor people, saying that ere long they should call me "madam"? And didst thou not kiss me, and bid me fetch thee thirty shillings? I put thee now to thy book-oath; deny it if thou canst. *(She weeps.)*

## *from* **The Merry Wives of Windsor** (II, i)

*Mistress Page, a wealthy dowager, has just received a love letter from the rascal Falstaff, who hopes to seduce her and get some money to pay his mounting debts. Mistress Page's reaction to the silly letter is a mixture of shock and flattery; although she does take delight in the "wicked" mischief that Falstaff proposes.*

**Mistress Page:** What, have I scaped love letters in the holiday time of my beauty, and am I now a subject for them? Let me see. *(She reads.)* "Ask me no reason why I love you, for though Love use Reason for his precision, he admits him not for his counsellor. You are not young; no more am I. Go to, then, there's sympathy. You are merry; so am I. Ha, ha, then, there's more sympathy. You love sack, and so do I. Would you desire better sympathy? Let it suffice thee, Mistress Page, at the least if the love of soldier can suffice, that I love thee. I will not say 'pity me' — 'tis not a soldier-like phrase — but I say 'love me' …

> By me, thine own true knight,
> By day or night
> Or any kind of light,
> With all his might
> For thee to fight,
> John Falstaff"

What a Herod of Jewry is this! O, wicked, wicked world! One that is well-night worn to pieces with age, to show himself a young gallant! What an unweighted behavior hath this Flemish drunkard picked, in the devil's name, out of my conversation, that he dares in this manner assay me? Why, he hath not been thrice in my company. What should I say to him? I was then frugal of my mirth, heaven forgive me. Why, I'll exhibit a bill in the Parliament for the putting down of men. O God, that I knew how to be revenged on him! For revenged I will be, as sure as his guts are made of pudding!

# *from* **A Midsummer Night's Dream** (I, i)

*Helena, a "tall blonde with no gift at all in shrewishness," is lamenting the complexities of her love life. She dreams of loving the handsome Demetrius, but he has jilted her for Hermia; and Hermia is her equally attractive, but shorter, best friend! To add to the complication, Hermia loves Lysander — the best friend of Demetrius — and they have both fled to the Athenian woods to escape the wrath of Hermia's father, who insists that she must marry Demetrius or suffer the alternative of death or life in a nunnery!*

**Helena:** How happy some o'er other some can be!
Through Athens I am thought as fair as she.
But what of that? Demetrius thinks not so;
He will not know what all but he do know.
And as he errs, doting on Hermia's eyes,
So I, admiring of his qualities.
Things base and vile, holding no quantity,
Love can transpose to form and dignity.
Love looks not with the eyes, but with the mind,
And therefore is a winged Cupid painted blind.
Nor hath love's mind of any judgement taste;
Wings and no eyes figure unheedy haste,
And therefore is love said to be a child
Because in choice he is so oft beguiled.
As waggish boys in game themselves forswear,
So the boy love is perjured everywhere;
For ere Demetrius looked on Hermia's eyne
He hailed down oaths that he was only mine,
And when this hail some heat from Hermia felt,
So he dissolved, and showers of oaths did melt.
I will go tell him of fair Hermia's flight.
Then to the wood will he tomorrow night
Pursue her; and for this intelligence
If I have thanks it is a dear expense.
But herein mean I to enrich my pain,
To have his sight thither, and back again.

## *from* **Venus and Adonis** (Lines 1112-1188)

*The immortal love story of Venus and Adonis is rich in dramatic performance potential for the monolog audition. There are a number of individual passages of emotional intensity and internal conflict that rival the more traditional Shakespeare dialog found in playscripts. Here, Venus mourns the death of Adonis and her own sensual passion.*

Thus was Adonis slain: He ran upon a boar with his sharp spear,
Who did not whet his teeth at him again, but by a kiss thought
To persuade him there: and nuzzling in his flank, the loving swine
Sheathed unaware the tusk in his soft groin.

But he is dead, and never did he bless my youth with his — the more
Am I accurst. Since thou art dead, lo, here I prophesy sorrow on love
Hereafter shall attend. It shall be waited on with jealousy, find sweet
Beginning, but an unsavory end to match his woe.

Poor flower, this was thy father's guise — sweet issue of a more sweet-
Smelling sire — for every little grief to wet his eyes. To grow unto himself
Was his desire, and so 'tis thine; but know, it is as good to wither in my
Loving breast as in his cold, cold blood.

Here was thy father's bed, here in my breast; thou are the next of blood,
And 'tis thy right. Lo, in this hollow cradle take thy rest; while betimes
My throbbing heart shall rock thee day and night. There shall not be
One minute in an hour wherein I will not kiss my sweet love's flower.

## *from* **The Taming of the Shrew** (IV, i)

*The dashing Petruchio has just returned home with his new wife, Katherina, who is notorious far and wide as a "shrew" with a devilish, unbridled spirit. Petruchio won the hand of the stubborn Katherina with a vow to "tame" her, and has set in motion a cunning plan to break "Kate" of her annoying habits and convert her into a proper wife. Here, he updates his progress in the taming of the shrew.*

**Petruchio:** Thus have I politicly begun my reign,
And 'tis my hope to end successfully.
My falcon now is sharp and passing empty,
And till she stoop she must not be full-gorged,
For then she never looks upon her lure.
Another way I have to man my haggard,
To make her come and know her keeper's call —
That is, to watch her as we watch these kites
That bate and beat, and will not be obedient.
She ate no meat today, no none shall eat.
Last night she slept not, nor tonight she shall not.
As with the meat, some undeserved fault
I'll find about the making of the bed,
And here she'll fling the pillow, there the bolster,
This way the coverlet, another way the sheets,
Ay, and amid this hurly I intend
That all is done in reverent care of her,
And in conclusion she shall watch all night,
And if she chance to nod I'll rail and brawl
And with the clamor keep her still awake.
This is the way to kill a wife with kindness,
And thus I'll curb her mad and headstrong humor.
He that knows better how to tame a shrew,
Now let him speak. 'Tis charity to show.

## CHAPTER FIVE
# PLAYING PERIOD MONOLOGS

*"The actor must become familiar with the entire past of*
*humanity...the manners, customs, and passions of different*
*peoples and of different times. Now, how can these sentiments*
*be embodied without dipping into books — for the past —*
*and into the current of life — for the present."*

— Tommaso Salvini

In playing "period" monologs it is important to capture the spirit of
the times in terms of mannerisms, lifestyles, and attitudes that reinforce
the accuracy and authenticity of the historical character portrait. The
contemporary appeal of the monologs included in this chapter is that
they provide alternative performance opportunities for the frequent
request to include a "non-modern," "non-classical" or "period"
monolog in the audition. There is also the immediate appeal of comic
satire, character exaggeration, and intriguing storylines that wring both
comedy and tragedy from the customs, manners, and beliefs of daily
life in past historical times as revealed by period characters.

Looked at from a performance perspective, however, playing
period monologs should suggest attention to historical detail in voicing
witty exchanges of dialog; executing elegant social graces or
movement; and exhibiting sophisticated behavior. That is why the actor
should research all of the information available regarding the historical
times and review materials related to social attitudes, conventions, or
mores as an integral part of the initial preparation for exploring the period
character portrait. For example, a review of the letters, diaries, or
chronicles of the historical times may provide invaluable insight related to
character intention, motivation, or point of view that could be integrated
into the audition performance to suggest believability and authenticity.

In the research role of private detective, the serious actor should consider documentary films, museum visits, portrait galleries, costume exhibitions, musical recitals, jewelry displays, antique shops, or even artifacts that help capture a glimpse of past historical times. This approach to playing period monologs may also lead to the delightful discovery of potential performance clues for characterization, interpretation, or even staging. These creative, informed research strategies should help the actor accurately visualize the historical time frame of the period monolog and also promote an atmosphere of authenticity and detail that captures the essential ingredients of the past in a more immediate and inventive audition performance. Little effort should be made, however, to imitate the historical times or to re-create the historical period in performance. Instead, the actor playing period monologs should cultivate only a tantalizing reflection of the many character foibles, idiosyncrasies, habits, or intrigues suggested in the selected monologs and dramatic narratives included in this chapter.

The demand for sharp, precise period characterization sometimes encourages an excess of spontaneity and zeal in portraying elegant social graces or historical customs; and it also cautions against undue caricature or distortion. Indeed, any excess or exaggeration that might suggest shallowness or superficiality should be avoided in playing period monologs. That is why it is crucial to practice moderation in the period audition performance; and to engage in direct and immediate characterization through the vocal delivery of the lines of the dialog rather than attempting a three-dimensional, complex character portrait that seeks to impose the historical times on the selected monologs.

At first, it may appear rather awkward or artificial to concentrate exclusively upon the voice and to engage in active word play with the dialog to punctuate period character development. But keep in mind that the majority of period playscripts are written in verse and require more attention to the rhythm and the meter of a character's spoken dialog than to movement or stylized gestures to communicate intention or motivation. Neglect of crisp, articulate speech in the period monolog can only lead to a ragged, unpolished delivery of the dialog that may not be clearly heard or understood by the audience. Voicing individual lines of verse that heighten poetic imagery and enrich the subtext, or hidden meaning, of the dialog also requires careful attention to physical control and posture. Learn to maintain a relaxed and yet alert posture with the individual parts of the body perfectly aligned to suggest a graceful, fluid period physicalization. The head should be held high and the arms should be relaxed at the side; and vocal sounds should be placed forward in the mouth to promote precise enunciation and crisp articulation of period dialog.

Although the dramatic critic Michel St. Denis assures us that, essentially, there is no difference in the performance approach to period or contemporary acting — "it's only that they do not take place on the same level" — playing period monologs is still considered non-realistic. Actors are often frankly theatrical and audience-centered in playing period monologs, with manners and movements that may appear dated, distracting, or unnatural in comparison to more familiar, contemporary performance practices. So, while it is very important to be aware of the historical influence of style in playing period monologs, it is much more important for the contemporary actor to discover an acting style that merely hints at the historical period. It is also important for the contemporary actor playing period monologs to feature a more "here-and-now" performance emphasis upon personal behavior, individual mannerisms, and inventive interpretation in sketching historical character portraits that are both imaginative and memorable.

As you now begin your rehearsal blueprint devoted to playing period monologs, it is essential to mirror the social customs, manners, and behavioral traits of historical characters as faithfully as possible without resorting to distortion or deceit. Your character portraits should exhibit sophisticated grace and elegance, economical and yet expressive physical gestures, musicality of voice, and disciplined, well-defined movement. Regularly scheduled rehearsal time is an excellent opportunity to explore historical music or dances that enrich your sense of stylized movement or staging. You may also use the rehearsal time to integrate appropriate stage business that promotes the effective use of period fans, walking sticks, snuff-boxes, spectacles, or handkerchiefs in enhancing the audition performance.

Regardless of the individual performance blueprint you choose to pursue in playing period monologs, it will be important in each selected monolog to exhibit ease and freedom of movement, to project vocal variety as well as vocal control, and to demonstrate an emotional and

111

intellectual honesty that is genuine and sincere. Leave nothing to random chance in sketching your historical portrait; and arm yourself with a strong sense of each monolog character's primary intention or motivation. It is important, also, to relate to the role you are playing; and to have a personal identification with the period circumstances, conflicts, or complications suggested in each monolog. Playing period characters in an open, honest, and sincere manner should transform the following unfamiliar historical stage figures into more contemporary flesh-and-blood men and women characters who will be easily recognized in an audition performance.

What remains for you in playing period monologs is to blend historical principles and personal, inventive performance practices into an artistic expression that accurately reflects and reinforces the heart and soul of the character portrait being drawn. Your identification and understanding of the actions and thoughts expressed in the following monologs should enhance the believability of the character portrait as well. Although you cannot hope to duplicate every element of the historical period as it is suggested in the monolog, careful selection and attention to significant details which help you visualize the character for yourself and for the audience provides a meaningful glimpse of the historical times in the rehearsal blueprint and the audition performance.

## *from* The School for Scandal (1777)
### (Richard Brinsley Sheridan)

*Sir Peter Teazle, a middle-aged gentleman of a stubborn and quarrelsome nature, has just recently married an innocent — and much younger — girl from the country. Although pleasant and gentle herself, Lady Teazle has become involved with a circle of vicious gossips and in trying to imitate their lifestyles has become very frivolous and careless in spending her husband's considerable fortune.*

**Sir Peter Teazle:** When an old bachelor takes a young wife, what is he to expect? 'Tis now six months since Lady Teazle made me the happiest of men — and I have been the miserablest dog ever since that ever committed wedlock! We tift a little going to church, and came to a quarrel before the bells were done ringing. I was more than once nearly choked with gall during the honeymoon, and had lost all comfort in life before my friends had done wishing me joy! Yet I chose with caution — a girl bred wholly in the country; who never knew luxury beyond one silk gown, nor dissipation above the annual gala of a race ball. Yet now she plays her part in all the extravagant fopperies of the fashion and the town; with as ready a grace as if she had never seen a bush nor a grass-plat out of Grosvenor Square! I am sneered at by my old acquaintances — paragraphed in the newspapers. She dissipates my fortune, and contradicts all my humors. Yet the worst of it is, I'm afraid I love her, or I should never bear all this. However, I'll never be weak enough to own it!

**Lady Teazle:** Sir Peter, Sir Peter. You may bear it not, as you please; but I ought to have my own way in everything. And what's more, I will, too! What? Though I was, of course, educated in the country, I know very well that women of fashion in London are accountable to nobody after they are married. If you wanted authority over me, you should have adopted me, not married me. I am sure you were old enough! My extravagance. I'm sure I'm not more extravagant than a woman of fashion ought to be. And am I to blame, Sir Peter, because flowers are so dear in cold weather? You should find fault with the climate, and not with me. For my part, I'm sure, I wish it was spring all the year round; and that roses grew under one's feet! What? Yes, I remember the curious life I led before meeting you. My daily occupation to inspect the dairy, superintend the poultry, make extracts from the family receipt-book — and comb my aunt Deborah's lapdog! For my part, I should think you would like to have your wife thought a woman of taste. But, I suppose, after having married you I should never pretend to taste again. But now, Sir Peter, if we have finished our daily jangle, I presume I may go to my engagement at Lady Sneerwell's. What? They are all people of rank and fortune, and remarkably tenacious of reputation. What? Would you restrain the freedom of speech! I vow that I bear no malice against the people I abuse. When I say an ill-natured thing, 'tis out of pure good humor; and I take it for granted they deal exactly in the same manner with me. But, Sir Peter, you know what you promised: to come to Lady Sneerwell's too. You must make haste after me, or you'll be too late. So, good-bye to you!

*Having fled her home several hours earlier, Lady Teazle now pays a visit to the notorious Lady Sneerwell, who is presiding over an afternoon meeting of the society gossips. The clan has gathered for the anticipated daily report of Mrs. Candour, a crusty old matron who delights in chronicling the current scandals and intrigues that are making the rounds of the city.*

**Mrs. Candour:** My dear Lady Sneerwell, how have you been this century? Mr. Surface, what news do you hear? — though indeed it is no matter, for I think one hears nothing else but scandal these days. Ah, Maria! Child — what, is the whole affair off between you and Charles? His extravagance, I presume — the town talks of nothing else. I own I was hurt to hear it, as indeed I was to learn, from the same quarter, that your guardian Sir Peter, and Lady Teazle have not agreed lately so well as could be wished. What's to be done? People will talk — there's no preventing it. Why, it was but yesterday I was told that Miss Gadabout had eloped with Sir Filigree Flirt. But, Lord! There's no minding what one hears — though, to be sure, I had this from very good authority. The world is so censorious, no character escapes. Now, who would have suspected your friend, Miss Prim, of an indiscretion? Yet such is the ill-nature of people, that they say her uncle stopped her last week, just as she was stepping into the York Diligence with her dancing master. But what's to be done, as I said before? How will you prevent people from talking? To be sure, tale-bearers are as bad as the tale-makers. Today, Mrs. Clackit assured me Mr. and Mrs. Honeymoon were at last become mere man and wife, like the rest of their acquaintances. She likewise hinted that a certain widow, in the next street, had got rid of her dropsy and recovered her shape in a most surprising manner. And at the same time Miss Tattle, who was by, affirmed that Lord Buffalo had discovered his lady at a house of no extraordinary fame — and that Sir Harry Bouquet and Tom Saunter were to measure swords on a similar provocation. But, Lord, do you think I would report these things! No, no! Tale-bearers, as I said before, are just as bad as tale-makers. I confess, Mr. Surface, I cannot bear to hear people attacked behind their backs; and when ugly circumstances come out against one's acquaintance, I own I always love to think the best. By the bye, I hope it is not true that your brother is absolutely ruined? But you must tell him to keep up his spirits — everybody almost is in the same way! Lord Spindle, Sir Thomas Splint, Captain Quinze, and Mr. Nickit — all up, I hear within this week. So, if Charles is undone, he'll find half his acquaintances ruined too — and that, you know, is a great consolation.

## from **The Misanthrope** (1666)
### (Molière)

*Alceste, a malcontent who has become so bitter about the hypocrisy and superficiality of the French court of Louis XIV that he wishes to withdraw from society, desperately loves the beautiful and enticing Celimene. Celimene, however, is very much a part of high society; and she enjoys teasing men with her affections. Here, Celimene responds to criticism that her reputation is in peril as a result of her questionable behavior.*

**Celimene:** Madam, I have a great many thanks to return you. Such counsel lays me under an obligation; and, far from taking it amiss, I intend this very moment to repay the favor, by giving you an advice which also touches *your* reputation closely. And as I see you prove yourself my friend by acquainting me with the stories that are current of me, I shall follow so nice an example by informing you what is said of you. In a house the other day, where I paid a visit, I met some people of exemplary merit who, while talking of the proper duties of a well-spent life, turned the topic of conversation upon you, Madam. There your prudishness and your too fervent zeal were not at all cited as a good example. This affectation of a grave demeanor, your eternal conversations on wisdom and honor, your mincings and mouthings at the slightest shadows of indecency, which an innocent though ambiguous word may convey, that lofty esteem in which you hold yourself, and those pitying glances which you cast upon all, your frequent lectures and your acid censures on things which are pure and harmless; all this, if I may speak frankly to you, Madam, was blamed unanimously. What is the good, said they, of this modest mien and this prudent exterior, which is belied by all the rest? She says her prayers with the utmost exactness; but she beats her servants and pays them no wages. She displays great fervor in every place of devotion; but she paints and wishes to appear handsome. She covers the nudities in her pictures; but loves the reality. As for me, I undertook your defense against everyone; and positively assured them that it was nothing but scandal. But the general opinion went against me, as they came to the conclusion that you would do well to concern yourself less about the actions of others, and take a little more pains with your own!

## *from* The Beggar's Opera (1728)
### (John Gay)

*This ballad opera popularized London low-life in the 18th century and set the stage for later heroic dramas and musicals that glamorized the lives of hardened criminals and vagabonds of the night. Macheath, fearless leader of a rowdy gang of cutthroats, loves his ale and his "street ladies" who display their social graces and lovely forms with such cunning and seductive artistry!*

**Macheath:** I must have women! There is nothing unbends the mind like them! Dear Mrs. Coaxer, you are welcome. You look charmingly today. I hope you don't want the repairs of quality, and lay on paint. Dolly Trull! Kiss me, hussy! Are you as amorous as ever? You are always so taken up with stealing hearts, that you don't allow yourself time to steal anything else. Ah, Dolly thou wilt ever be a coquette. Mrs. Vixen, I'm yours! I always loved a woman of wit and spirit. They make charming mistresses, but plaguey wives. Oh, Betty Doxy! Come hither, turtledove. Do you drink as hard as ever? You had better stick to good wholesome beer; for in troth, Betty, strong waters will in time ruin your constitution. You should leave those to your betters. What! And my pretty Jenny Diver too! As prim and demure as ever! There is not any prude, though ever so high bred, hath a more sanctified look; but with a more mischievous heart! Ah! Thou art a dear artful hypocrite, Mrs. Slammekin! As careless and genteel as ever! All you fine ladies, you know your own beauty. But see, here's Suky Tawdry come to contradict what I was saying. Everything she gets one way, she lays out and then back. Why, Suky, you must keep at least a dozen tally-men. Molly Brazen! *(Throws her a kiss.)* That's well done! I love a free-hearted wench. Thou hast a most agreeable assurance, girls; and art as willing as a turtle. But hark! I hear music. The harper is at the door. "If music be the food of love, play on!" Ere you seat yourselves, ladies, what think you of a dance?

*Later, when Macheath is fleeing from arrest and possible imprisonment, his sweetheart bemoans his fate; and her own fears of not being able to see him again. Here, the devoted and romantic Polly — who has that rare gift for believing and accepting — grows impatient for the return of the unpredictable Macheath.*

**Polly:** Now I'm a wretch, indeed. Methinks I see him already in the cart, sweeter and more lovely than the nosegay in his hand! I hear the crowd extolling his resolution and intrepidity! What volleys of sighs are sent from the widows of Holborn, that so comely a youth should be brought to disgrace. I see him at the tree! The whole circle are in tears — even butchers weep! Jack Ketch the hangman himself hesitates to perform his duty; and would be glad to lose his fee by a reprieve. What, then, will become of Polly? As yet I may inform him of their design, and aid him in his escape. It shall be so. But then he flies, absents himself, and I bar myself from his dear, dear conversation! That too will distract me. If he keep out of the way, my papa and mama may in time relent; and we may be happy. If he stays, he is hanged. And then he is lost forever! He intended to lie concealed in my room, till the dusk of the evening. If they are abroad, I'll this instant let him out lest some accident should prevent him.

## *from* **Cyrano de Bergerac** (1897)
### (Edmond Rostand)

*The honest, courageous, and romantic Cyrano is a brilliant musician, talented poet, agile swordsman, and philosopher in 17th-century France. There is only one apparent, singular defect in his otherwise perfect person: an* enormous *nose that provokes laughter, disgust, and ridicule. This deformity, however, has inspired the biting wit and daring insolence which arms him against the dull and ordinary who dare to confront his nose extraordinaire!*

**Cyrano:**             Take notice, boobies all.
Who finds my visage's center ornament

117

A thing to jest at — that it is my wont —
An if the jester's noble — ere we part
To let him taste my steel, and not my boot!
Know that I am proud possessing such appendice.
'Tis well known, a big nose is indicative
Of a soul affable, and kind, and courteous,
Liberal, brave, just like myself, and such
As you can never dare to dream yourself,
Rascal contemptible! Show your heels, now!
Or tell me why you stare so at my nose!
Well, what is there so strange to the eye?
How now? Is't soft and dangling, like a bird?
Is it crook'd, like an owl's beak?
Do you see a wart upon the tip? Or a fly,
That takes the air there? What is there to stare at?
You might have said a thousand things, like this, by
Varying the tone. Aggressive: "Sir, if I had such a nose
I'd amputate it!" Friendly: "When you sup it must annoy
You, dipping in your cup; and you must need a special shape!"
Descriptive: "'Tis a rock!…a peak!…a cape!
A cape! Forsooth! 'Tis a peninsula!"
Gracious: "You love the little birds, I think?
I see you've managed with a fond research
To find their tiny claws a roomy perch!"
Considerate: "Take care, with your head bowed low
By such a weight, lest head o'er heels you go!"
Tender: "Pray get a small umbrella made,
Lest its bright color in the sun should fade!"
Cavalier: "The last fashion, friend, that hook?
To hang your hat on? 'Tis a useful crook!"
Emphatic: "No wind, O majestic nose,
Can give *thee* cold — save when the mistral blows!"
Dramatic: "When it bleeds, what a Red Sea!"
Admiring: "Sign for a perfumery!"
Simple: "When is the monument on view?"
Rustic: "Call that thing a nose? Ay, marry, no!
'Tis a dwarf pumpkin, or a prize turnip!"

Military: "Point against cavalry!"
Practical: "Put it in the lottery!
Assuredly 'twould be the biggest prize!"
Or, parodying the lover Pyramus' sighs,
"Behold the nose that mars the harmony
Of its master's phiz! blushing its treachery!"
Such, my dear sir, is what you might have said,
Had you the least of wit or letters.
But, of wit you have not an atom, and of letters
There are only three that spell *you* out — A - S - S!

## *from* **The Importance of Being Earnest** (1895)

### (Oscar Wilde)

*Two attractive, sophisticated young ladies in polite society are being pursued by equally handsome, refined young men. The two young ladies, however, feel that they cannot marry anyone who is not named Earnest. Gwendolen, one of the young ladies who is infatuated with the extravagant Jack, discovers that her best friend, Cecily, is actually Jack's ward; and that seriously threatens the social friendship of the young ladies.*

**Gwendolen:** Oh! It is strange he never mentioned to me that he had a ward. How secretive of him! He grows more interesting hourly. I am not sure, however, that the news inspires me with feelings of unmixed delight. *(Rising and going to her)* I am very fond of you, Cecily: I have liked you ever since I met you! But I am bound to state that now that I know that you are Mr. Worthing's ward, I cannot help expressing a wish you were — well, just a little older than you seem to be — and not quite so very alluring in appearance. In fact, if I may speak candidly — *(Pause)* Well, to speak with perfect candor, Cecily, I wish that you were fully forty-two, and more than usually plain for your age. Ernest has a strong, upright nature. He is the very soul of truth and honor. Disloyalty would be as impossible to him as deception. But even men of the noblest possible moral character are extremely susceptible to the influence of the physical charms of others. Modern, no less than Ancient History, supplies us with many most painful examples of what I refer to. If it were not so, indeed, History would be quite unreadable.

If the poor fellow has been entrapped into any foolish promise I shall consider it my duty to rescue him at once, and with a firm hand.

## *from* **Life Is a Dream** (1635)
### (Pedro Calderon)

*The young prince Segismundo has been imprisoned in a tower by his father, who fears a soothsayer's dire predictions about his son's future. Chained and clad in tattered rags, Segismundo lives the life of a caged animal. In his constant agony, the young prince now yearns for his lost freedom and liberty.*

**Segismundo:** Oh, wretch that I am! Oh, unfortunate! I try, of heavens, to understand, since you treat me so, what crime I committed against you when I was born…but, since I was born, I understand my crime. Your cruel justice has had sufficient cause. For man's greatest crime is to have been born at all. Still, I should like to know, to ease my anxiety — leaving aside, ye gods, the sin of being born — in what way I could offend you any more, to deserve more punishment? Were not all other men born too? If so, why do they have blessings that I never enjoyed? The bird is born, with the gaudy plumage that gives it unrivaled beauty; and scarcely is it formed, like flower of feathers or a winged branch, when it swiftly cuts the vaulted air, refusing the calm shelter of its nest. But I, with more soul, have less liberty! The beast is born, too, with skin beautifully marked, like a cluster of stars — thanks to Nature's skilled brush; then stern necessity, cruel and savage, teaches it to be cruel also, and it reigns a monster in its labyrinth. Yet I, with better instincts, have less liberty! The fish is born, unbreathing, a creature of spawn and seaweed, and scarcely is it seen — a scaly vessel in the waves — when it darts in so many directions, measuring the vastness of the cold and the deep. And I, with more free will, I have less liberty! The stream is born, a snake uncoiling among the flowers, and scarcely does this serpent of silver break through the blossoms, when it celebrates their grace with music, and with music takes its passage through the majesty of the open plain. Yet I, who have more life, have less liberty! As I reach this pitch of anger, like a volcano, an Aetna, I could tear pieces of my heart from my own breast. What law, justice, or reason, can deny to man so sweet a privilege, so elementary a freedom, as God has given to a brook, a fish, a beast, and a bird?

## *from* **The Miser** (1668)

### (Molière)

*The French comedy of manners delights in ridiculing trifle customs and human nature that is pretentious and hypocritical. In this monolog, Harpagon (the Miser) is enraged when he discovers that the secret, buried treasure he worships has been unearthed and that he is now penniless!*

**Harpagon:** Stop thief! Stop thief! Stop assassin! Stop murderer! Justice! Divine justice! I am ruined! I've been murdered! He cut my throat, he stole my money! Who can it be? What's become of him? Where is he? Where is he hiding? What shall I do to find him? Where shall I run? Where shall I not run? Isn't that he there? Isn't this he here? Who's this? *(Sees his own shadow and grabs his own arm.)* Stop! Give me back my money, you rogue. Ah! It is myself! My mind is unhinged, and I don't know where I am, who I am, or what I am doing. *(Falls to his knees.)* Alas! My poor money, my poor money, my dear friend, they have taken you from me. And since they carried you off, I've lost my support, my consolation, my joy. Everything is at an end for me; I have no more to do in this world! I cannot live without you! It's finished. I can do no more. *(Lies down.)* I am dying. I am dead. I am buried! Isn't there anybody who would like to bring me back to life by returning my dear money or by telling me who took it? *(Rising to his knees)* What did you say? It was nobody. *(Stands.)* Whoever did the job must have watched very closely for his chance; for he chose exactly the time when I was talking to my treacherous son. *(Takes his hat and cane.)* I'll go and demand justice. I'll order them to torture everyone in my house for a confession: the maids, the valets, my son, my own daughter — and myself too! What a crowd of people! Everybody I cast my eyes on arouses my suspicion, and everything seems to be the thief. Eh! What are you talking about there? About the man that robbed me? Why are you making that noise up there? Is my thief there? *(Kneels and addresses the audience.)* Please, if anyone has any information about my thief, I beg you to tell me. Are you sure he isn't hidden there among

you? They all look at me and laugh. *(Stands.)* You will probably see
that they all had a part in this robbery. Here, quick, commissaries,
archers, provosts, judges, tortures, scaffolds, and executioners! I want
to have everybody hanged! And if I don't recover my money, I'll hang
myself afterward!

## *from* **The Beaux' Stratagem** (1707)

### (George Farquahar)

*The English 18th-century comedy of manners offers a vivid reflection of
witty, sentimental characters who reveal themselves as unnaturally good,
especially in pathetic situations. In the monolog that follows, Mrs. Sullen
discusses marriage and the proper conduct one should observe in polite
society.*

**Mrs. Sullen:** Country pleasures! Racks and torments! Dost think,
child, that my limbs were made for leaping ditches, and clambering
over stiles? Or that my parents, wisely foreseeing my future happiness
in country pleasures, had early instructed me in the rural
accomplishments of drinking fat ale, playing at whist, and smoking
tobacco with my husband? Or of spreading of plasters, brewing of diet-
drinks, and stilling rosemary-water, with the good old gentlewoman,
my mother-in-law? Not that I disapprove of rural pleasures, as the poets
have painted them; in their landscape, every Phyllis has her Corydon,
every murmuring stream, and every flow'ry mead, gives fresh alarums
to love. Besides, you'll find that their couples were never married. But
yonder I see my Corydon, and a sweet swain he is, heaven knows!
Come, Dorinda, don't be angry, he's my husband, and your brother;
and, between them both, is he not a sad brute? O Sister, Sister! If ever
you marry, beware of a sullen, silent sot, one that's always musing, but
never thinks. There's some diversion in a talking blockhead; and since
a woman must wear chains, I would have the pleasure of hearing 'em
rattle a little. Now you shall see, but take this by the way. He came
home this morning at his usual hour of four, wakened me out of a sweet
dream of something else by tumbling over the tea-table, which he broke
all to pieces. After his man and he had rolled about the room like sick
passengers in a storm, he comes flounce into bed, dead as a salmon into

a fishmonger's basket; his feet cold as ice, his breath hot as a furnace, and his hands and his face as greasy as his flannel night-cap. O, matrimony! He tosses up the clothes with a barbarous swing over his shoulders, disorders the whole economy of my bed, leaves me half naked, and my whole night's comfort is the tuneable serenade of that wakeful nightingale, his nose! Oh, the pleasure of counting the melancholy clock by a snoring husband! But now, Sister, you shall see how handsomely, being a well-bred man, he will beg my pardon.

## *from* **Volpone** (1606)

### (Ben Jonson)

*Volpone, "the fox," is a sly and lustful braggard who feigns illness to trick his greedy friends into promising him their wealth in the hope of inheriting his vast estate and fortune when he dies. One of the greedy friends even pledges his wife, Celia, to secure Volpone's favor. Here, Volpone tries to seduce the innocent Celia with an elaborate and deceptive declaration of love.*

**Volpone:** Nay, fly me not.
　　Nor let thy false imagination
　　That I was bed-rid, make thee think I am so:
　　Thou shalt not find it. I am now as fresh,
　　As hot, as high, and in as jovial plight
　　As, when, in that so celebrated scene,
　　At recitation of our comedy,
　　For entertainment of the great Valois,
　　I acted young Antinous; and attracted
　　The eyes and ears of all the ladies present.
　　To admire each graceful gesture, note, and footing.
　　*(Sings.)* "Come, my Celia, let us prove
　　　　While we can, the sports of love,
　　　　Time will not be ours forever,
　　　　Why should we defer our joys?
　　　　'Tis no sin love's fruits to steal:
　　　　But the sweet thefts to reveal."

\*　　　\*　　　\*　　　\*

Why droops my Celia?
Thou hast, in the place of a base husband found
A worthy lover: use thy fortune well,
With secrecy and pleasure. See, behold,
What thou art queen of; not in expectation,
As I feed others: but processed and crowned.
The heads of parrots, tongues of nightingales,
The brains of peacocks, and of ostriches,
Shall be our food, and, could we get the phoenix,
Though nature lost her kind, she were our dish.
If thou hast wisdom, hear me, Celia.
And I will meet thee in as many shapes;
Where we may so transfuse our wandering souls
Out at our lips, and score up sums of pleasures.

## *from* The Ghost Sonata (1907)

### (August Strindberg)

*Set in a kind of limbo, or purgatory, where humans are doomed forever to wander aimlessly until they reach the peaceful realm of the dead, the evil Old Man seeks vengeance on a number of nameless inhabitants. There is an air of mystery and uncertainty about the Old Man, who scorns the world but here exposes the deceit and betrayal of the inhabitants he meets in an abandoned house.*

**Old Man:** Should we talk about the weather? Ask each other how we're feeling? I prefer silence...in which one can hear thoughts and see the past. Silence cannot hide anything — which is more than you can say for words. Extraordinary, how silent you all are! Take this house, for example. All of us sitting here, we know who we are, don't we? I don't have to tell you...And you know me although you pretend ignorance. Sitting in that room is my daughter, yes mine, and you know that, too. She has lost all desire to live, without knowing why. She was withering away because of the air in this house, which reeks of crime, deception, and deceits of every kind. That is why I had to find a friend for her, a friend from whose very presence she would apprehend the warmth and light radiated by a noble deed. That was my mission in this house. To pull up the weeds, to expose the crimes, to settle the accounts, so that these young people might make a new beginning in this home; which is my gift of life to them. Listen to the ticking of the clock, like a deathwatch beetle in the wall! Listen to what it's saying…"time's up, time's up!" When it strikes — in just a few more moments — your time is up. Then you may go — not before. But the clock raises its arm before it strikes. Listen! It's warning you…"Clocks can strike!" And I can strike, too! Do you understand?

## *from* **The Octoroon** (1859)

### (Dion Boucicault)

*The beautiful but socially inferior Zoe is secretly in love with George Peyton, who owns Terrebone Plantation. But the wealthy Dora Sunnyside is also in love with the handsome plantation owner, and asks Zoe to plead her case to George. When George confesses that he has loved Zoe from the moment he saw her, she is forced to reveal a terrible secret that threatens their future happiness.*

**Zoe:** *(Aside)* Alas, he does not know, he does not know! and will despise me, spurn me, loathe me, when he learns who, what, he has so loved. *(Aloud)* George, you cannot marry me; the laws forbid it! There is a gulf between us, as wide as your love, as deep as my despair. But tell me, tell me you will pity me! That you will not throw me from you like a poisoned thing! What shall I say? I — my mother was — no, not her! Why should I refer the blame to her? George, do you see that hand you hold? Look at these fingers. Do you see the nails are of a bluish tinge? Look in my eyes; is not the same color in the white? Could you see the roots of my hair you would see the same dark, fatal mark. Do you know what that is? It is the eternal curse of Cain. Of the blood that feeds my heart, one drop in eight is black. Bright red as the rest may be, that one drop poisons all the flood; those seven bright drops give me love like yours — hope like yours — ambition like yours — life hung with passions like dew drops on the morning flowers. But the one black drop gives me despair, for I'm an unclean thing — forbidden by the laws — I'm…I'm…Yes, I'd rather be black than ungrateful! Oh, George, our race has at least one virtue — it knows how to suffer!

## *from* **All for Love** (1677)

### (John Dryden)

*This elegant blank verse re-telling of William Shakespeare's* Antony and Cleopatra *here presents the lovely, seductive Cleopatra at her most cunning and dramatic. Surrounded by armed soldiers, she pleads a daring defense as well as an arrogant dismissal of Mark Antony's decision to leave her and return to Rome.*

**Cleopatra:**             Yet may I speak?
How shall I plead my cause, when you, my judge,
Already have condemn'd me?
                   Shall I bring
The love you bore me for my advocate?
That now is turn'd against me, that destroys me;
For love, once past, is at the best forgotten;
But oft'ner sours to hate.
                 'Twill please my lord
To ruin me, and therefore I'll be guilty.
But, could I once have thought it would have pleas'd you,
That you would pry, with narrow searching eyes,
Into my faults, severe to my destruction,
And watching all advantages with care,
That serve to make me wretched?
                 You seem griev'd
(And therein you are kind) that Caesar first
Enjoy'd my love, though you deserv'd it better.
I grieve for that, my lord, much more than you;
For, had I first been yours, it would have sav'd
My second choice: I never have been his,
And ne'er had been but yours. But Caesar first,
You say, possess'd my love. Not so, my lord:
He first possess'd my person, you, my love:
Caesar lov'd me, but I lov'd Antony.
If I endur'd him after, 'twas because
I judg'd it due to the first name of men;
And, half constrain'd, I gave, as to a tyrant,

What he would take by force.
How often have I wish'd some other Caesar,
Great as the first, and as the second young,
Would court my love, to be refus'd for you!
you leave me, Antony; and yet I love you,
Indeed I do: I have refus'd a kingdom —
That's a trifle:
For I could part with life, with anything,
But only you.
                              Oh, let me die with you!
Is that a hard request?
No, you shall go; your int' rest calls you hence;
Yes, your dear int' rest pulls too strong, for these
Weak arms to hold you here.
                              Go! Leave me, soldier
For you're no more a lover; and leave me dying:
Push me pale and panting from your bosom,
And, when your march begins, let one run after,
Breathless almost for joy, and cry, "She's dead."
The soldiers shout; you then, perhaps, may sigh,
And muster all your Roman gravity:
Ventidius chides; and straight your brow clears up,
As I had never been.
Here let me breathe my last: envy me not
This minute; I'll die apace,
As fast as e'er I can, and end your trouble.

## *from* **The Historical Register** (1736)

### (Henry Fielding)

*The social satire and biting parody of this narrative lies in its suggestion that heroic and honorable intangibles like "political honesty" and "patriotism" are commodities that are regularly for sale on the auction block. The Auctioneer, however, appears to maintain his decorum and sense of urgency in spite of the satirical point of view.*

**Auctioneer:** I dare swear, gentlemen and ladies, this auction will give general satisfaction. It is the first of its kind which I ever had the honor to exhibit, and I believe I may even challenge the world to produce some of the curiosities which this choice cabinet contains. Gentlemen and ladies, this is Lot 1: a most curious remnant of political honesty. Who puts it up gentlemen? It will make you a very good cloak. you see it's both sides alike, so you may turn it as often as you will. Come — five pounds for this curious remnant. I assure you, several great men have made their birthday suits out of the same piece. It will wear forever and never be the worse for wearing. Five pounds is bid. Nobody more than five pounds for this curious piece of political honesty? Five pound. No more? *(Knocks.)* Sold to Lord Both Sides. Lot 2. A most delicate piece of patriotism, gentlemen. Who bids? Ten pounds for this piece of patriotism? Sir, I assure you several gentlemen at court have worn the same. 'Tis a quite different thing within to what it is without. You take it for the old patriotism, whereas it is indeed like that in nothing but the cut; but, alas, sir, there is a great difference in the stuff. But, sir, I don't propose this for a town suit. This is only proper for the country. Consider, gentlemen, what a figure this will make at an election. Come — five pound? One guinea? *(Silence)* Put patriotism aside. Lot 3. Three grains of modesty. Come, ladies, consider how scarce this valuable commodity is. Half a crown for all this modesty? Is there not one lady in the room who wants any modesty? It serves mighty well to blush behind a fan with, or to wear under a lady's mask at a masquerade. *(Silence)* What? Nobody bid? Well, lay modesty aside.

## *from* The Contrast (1787)

### (Royall Tyler)

*In this early American comedy of manners, the pretentious Dimple has just returned from Europe loaded down with the latest affectation and fashion, a scorn of all things American, and a considerable bill of debt. He also intends to cancel his marriage contract with the affable Maria to marry a wealthy woman. Although Maria does not yet know of Dimple's intentions, she has her own doubts about the impending marriage.*

**Maria:** How deplorable is my situation! How distressing for a daughter to find her heart militating with her filial duty! I know my father loves me tenderly. Why then do I very reluctantly obey him? Heaven knows! With what reluctance I should oppose the will of a parent, or set an example of filial disobedience. At a parent's command I could wed awkwardness and deformity. Were the heart of my husband good, I would so magnify his good qualities with the eye of conjugal affection, that the defects of his person and manners should be lost in the emanation of his virtues. At a father's command, I could embrace poverty. Were the poor man my husband, I would learn resignation to my lot. I would enliven our frugal meal with good humor, and chase away misfortune from our cottage with a smile. At a father's command, I could almost submit to what every female heart knows to be the most mortifying — to marry a weak man, and blush at my husband's folly in every company I visited. But to marry a depraved wretch, whose only virtue is a polished exterior; who is actuated by the unmanly ambition of conquering the defenseless; whose heart, insensible to the emotions of patriotism, dilates at the plaudits of every unthinking girl; and whose laurels are the sighs and tears of the miserable victims of his specious behavior! Can he, who has no regard for the peace and happiness of other families, ever have a due regard for the peace and happiness of his own? Would to heaven that my father were not so hasty in his temper! Surely, if I were to state my reasons for declining this match, he would not compel me to marry such a man — whom, though my lips may solemnly promise to honor, I find my heart must ever despise.

## *from* **The Cherry Orchard** (1904)

### (Anton Chekhov)

*Anton Chekhov's playscripts occupy a very unique place in the history of period theatre because they provide character portraits that are three-dimensional and matchless in their subtle emotional and intellectual dimension. Here, the poor but idealistic Trofimov expresses his point of view on human nature and politics as they are reflected in Czarist Russia on the verge of the 20th century.*

**Trofimov:** Humanity progresses, perfecting its powers. Everything that is beyond its ken now will one day become familiar and comprehensible. Only we must work; we must with all our powers aid the seeker after truth. Here among us in Russia the workers are few in number as yet. The vast majority of the intellectual people I know seek nothing, do nothing, and are not fit as yet for work of any kind. They call themselves intellectual, but they treat their servants as inferiors; behave to the peasants as though they were animals; learn little, read nothing seriously, do practically nothing, only talk about science, and know very little about art. They are all serious people, they all have severe faces, and they all talk of weighty matters and air their theories. And yet, the vast majority of us — ninety-nine percent — live like savages. At the least thing we fly to blows and abuse, eat piggishly, sleep in filth and stuffiness; with bugs everywhere, stench and damp and moral impurity. And it's clear all our fine talk is only to divert our attention and other people's. Show me where to find the creches there's so much talk about, and the reading-rooms? They only exist in the novels; in real life there are none of them. There is nothing but filth and vulgarity and apathy. I fear and dislike very serious faces. I'm afraid of serious conversations. We should do better to be silent.

## *from* **The Sea Gull** (1896)

(Anton Chekhov)

*The impending sense of doom and despair that Chekhov expressed as the dark clouds of revolution swirled over Russia is also evident in the character of Nina, who left home to find success on the stage but found failure instead. Here she unburdens herself to the young, sensitive writer who still loves her deeply in spite of her attraction for another man.*

**Nina:** Why do you say you kiss the ground I walk on? I ought to be killed. I'm so tired. If I could rest — rest. I'm a sea gull. No, that's not it. I'm an actress. Well, no matter now. He didn't believe in the theatre; all my dreams he'd laugh at and little by little I quit believing in it myself, and lost heart. And there was the strain of love, jealousy, constant anxiety about my little baby. I got to be small and trashy, and played without thinking. I didn't know what to do with my hands, couldn't stand properly on the stage, and couldn't control my voice. You can't imagine the feeling when you are acting and know it's dull. I'm a sea gull. No, that's not it. That's not it. *(Puts her hand to her forehead)* What was I? I — I was talking about the stage. Now I'm not like that. I'm a real actress. I act with delight, with rapture. I'm drunk when I'm on the stage; and feel that I am beautiful. And now, ever since I've been here, I've kept walking about; keep walking and thinking, thinking and even believing my soul grows stronger every day. Now I know, I understand that in our work — acting or writing — what matters is not fame, not glory, and not what I used to dream about. It's how to endure, to bear my cross, and to have faith. I have faith and it all doesn't hurt me so much. And when I think of my calling, I'm not afraid of life.

*Even the well-established and respected artist and intellectual Trigorin has become a jaded man of letters, unable to fully appreciate his talents or to understand his success. His personal frustration and frequent fits of despair are symptomatic of the unheroic characters he imagines in his own novels and short stories.*

**Trigorin:** You talk of fame and happiness, of bright, interesting life; but to me all those fine words, if you will forgive me saying so, are just like a sweetmeat which I never taste. I am haunted day and night by one persistent thought: I ought to be writing, I ought to be writing. I have scarcely finished one novel when, for some reason, I must begin writing another, then a third, and after that a fourth. I write incessantly, post haste, and I can't write in any other way. Oh, it is an absurd life! Here I see a cloud that looks like a grand piano. I say to myself that I must put into a story somewhere that a cloud sailed by that looked like a grand piano. I hurriedly make a note; a sickly smell, a widow's color, to be mentioned in the description of a summer evening. When I finish work I race off to the theatre or go fishing; if only I could rest in that and forget myself. And I have no rest from myself; and I feel that I am eating up my own life, and that for the sake of the honey I give to someone in space I am stripping the pollen from my best flowers; tearing up the flowers themselves and trampling on their roots. Do you think I am mad? Do my friends and acquaintances treat me as though I were sane? "What are you writing at now?" "What are you going to give us now?" It seems to me as though my friends' notice, their praises, their enthusiasm — that it's all a sham, that they are deceiving me as an invalid and I am somehow afraid that they will steal up to me from behind, snatch me, carry me off and put me in a madhouse! I have not seen my readers, but for some reason I have always imagined them to be hostile and mistrustful. I was afraid of the public. It alarmed me, and when I had to produce my first play it always seemed to me that all the dark people felt hostile; and all the fair ones were coldly indifferent. Oh, how awful it was! What agony it was!

## *from* **Doctor Faustus** (1587)

### (Christopher Marlowe)

*The Faust legend of a man who sells his soul to the devil in exchange for worldly pleasures, knowledge, and wealth is a deeply moving one that continues to interest us today. In this account of the temptation of Dr. Faustus, there is a great deal of sympathy and compassion at the climactic moment when Faustus must pay with his immortal soul for the diabolical aid he has accepted from the devil.*

**Faustus:**                O, Faustus!
Now hast thou but one bare hour to live
And then thou must be damned perpetually.
Stand still, you ever-moving spheres of Heaven
That time may cease and midnight never come.
Fair nature's eye, rise, rise again and make
Perpetual day, or let this hour be but a year,
A month, a week, a natural day —
That Faustus may repent and save his soul.
O, I'll leap up to my God! Who pulls me down?
See, see where Christ's blood streams in the firmament!
One drop of blood will save me. O, my Christ!
You stars that reigned at my nativity,
Now draw up Faustus like a foggy mist,
But let my soul mount and ascend to heaven.

O, half the hour is passed! 'Twill all be passed anon.
If thou wilt not have mercy on my soul
Yet for Christ's sake, whose blood hath ransomed me,
Impose some end to my incessant pain!
Let Faustus live in hell a thousand years,
A hundred thousand, and at last be saved!
*(The clock strikes twelve.)*
It strikes, it strikes! Now body, turn to air;
Or Lucifer will bear thee quick to hell!
O soul, be changed into small water-drops
And fall into the ocean, ne'er to be found.
*(Thunder and lightning)*
My God, my God! Look not so fierce on me!
Adders and serpents, let me breathe awhile.
Ugly Hell, gape not! Come not, Lucifer!
I'll burn my books! — O, Mephistopheles!

## *from* **There Shall Be No Night** (1940)

### (Robert E. Sherwood)

*Miranda is reading the last letter written by her husband, a lifelong pacifist, who finally realized the price one must pay for liberty. The husband, it appears, gave his own life in the pursuit of freedom after he received news of the death of his only son, Erik, who was killed defending his homeland of Finland against a Russian invasion.*

**Miranda:** *(Reading)* "In this time of our own grief it is not easy to summon up the philosophy which has been formed from long study of the sufferings of others. But I must do it, and you must help me. You see, he wanted to make me feel that I'm stronger — wiser. I have often read the words which Pericles spoke over the bodies of the dead, in the dark hour when the light of Athenian democracy was being extinguished by the Spartans. He told the mourning people that he could not give them any of the old words which tell how fair and noble it is to die in battle. Those empty words were old, even then, twenty-four centuries ago. But he urged them to find revival in the memory of the commonwealth which they together had achieved; and he promised them that the story of their commonwealth would never die; but would live on, far away, woven into the fabric of other men's lives. I believe that these words can be said now of our own dead, and our own commonwealth. I have always believed in the mystic truth of the Resurrection. The great leaders of the mind and the spirit — Socrates, Christ, Lincoln — were all done to death that the full measure of their contribution to human experience might never be lost. Now — the death of our son is only a fragment in the death of our country. But Erik and the others who gave their lives are also giving to mankind a symbol — a little symbol, to be sure, but a clear one — of man's unconquerable aspiration to dignity, freedom, and purity in the sight of God. When I made that radio speech — you remember? — I quoted from St. Paul. I repeat those words to you now, darling. 'We glory in tribulations; knowing that tribulation worketh patience; and patience, experience; and experience, hope.' There are men here from all different countries. Fine men. Those Americans who were at our house on New Year's Day — and that nice Polish officer, Major Rutkowski — they are all here. They are waiting for me now, so I must close this, with all my love."

## *from* **The Rivals** (1775)
### (Richard Brinsley Sheridan)

*The "high comedy" of the eighteenth century gave color and authenticity to social commentary that instructed one in customs and manners of the day. The dialog was often witty and inspirational; an ingenious arrangement of words that produces merriment and biting satire. In this monolog, Mrs. Malaprop — who has a problem with the ridiculous misuse of words, especially through confusion caused by resemblance in sound — lectures Sir Anthony on her understanding of a young girl's proper education.*

**Mrs. Malaprop:** Observe me, Sir Anthony. I would by no means wish a daughter of mine to be a progeny of learning. I don't think so much learning becomes a young woman; for instance — I would never let her meddle with Greek, or Hebrew, or Algebra, or Simony, or Fluxions, or Paradoxes, or such inflammatory branches of learning. Neither would it be necessary for her to handle any of your mathematical, astronomical, or diabolical instruments. But, Sir Anthony, I would send her, at nine years old, to a boarding school in order to learn a little ingenuity and artifice. Then, Sir, she should have a supercilious knowledge in accounts. And as she grew up, I would have her instructed in geometry that she might know something of the contagious countries. But above all, Sir Anthony, she should be mistress of orthodoxy; that she might not misspell and mispronounce words so shamefully as girls usually do. And likewise that she might reprehend the true meaning of what she is saying. This, Sir Anthony, is what I would have a woman know — and I don't think there is a superstitious article in it!

## *from* **Miss Julie** (1888)

### (August Strindberg)

*There is an intense, erotic struggle taking place between the fragile but frustrated Miss Julie and her rugged, sensual servant Jean. Following a festive Midsummer's Night town celebration, the privileged Miss Julie and the brutal Jean play out their roles of servant and master to reveal their own deeply troubled and psychologically flawed interiors.*

**Jean:** You lackey lover! You bootblack's tramp! Shut your mouth and get out of here! Who do you think you are telling me I'm coarse? I've never seen anybody of my class behave as crudely as you did tonight. Have you ever seen any of the girls around here grab a man like you did? Do you think any of the girls of my class would throw themselves at a man like that? I've never seen the like of it except in animals and prostitutes. I never hit a person who's down, especially a woman. I can't deny that, in one way, it was good to find that what I find glittering up above was only fool's gold; to see that the eagle's back was as gray as its belly; that the smooth cheek was just powder, and that there could be dirt under the manicured nails; that the handkerchief was soiled even though it smelled of perfume. But, in another way, it hurts to find that everything I was striving for wasn't very high above me after all; wasn't even real. It hurts me to see you sink far lower than your own cook. Hurts, like seeing the last flowers cut to pieces by the autumn rains and turned to muck. I'm sorry I said that. I'd be doing myself an injustice if I didn't admit that part of the credit for this seduction belongs to me. But do you think a person in my position would have dared to look twice at you if you hadn't asked for it? I'm still amazed — but it's no crime for a child to steal a few ripe cherries when they're falling off the tree, is it?

**Miss Julie:** Kill me! You can kill an innocent creature without turning a hair — then kill me. Oh, how I hate you! I loathe you! There's blood between us. I curse the moment I first laid eyes on you! I curse the moment I was conceived in my mother's womb. You don't think I can stand the sight of blood, do you? You think I'm so weak, don't you? Oh, how I'd like to see your blood, your brains on that chopping block. I'd love to see the whole of your sex swimming in a sea of blood. I could drink blood out of your skull. Use your chest as a foot bath, dip my toes in your guts! I could eat your heart roasted whole! You think I'm weak? You think I want to carry your blood under my heart and feed it with my blood? Bear your child and take your name? Come to think of it, what is your name? I've never even heard your last name. I'll bet you don't even have one. I'd be Mrs. Doorman or Madame Garbageman. You dog with *my* name on your collar — you lackey with *my* initials on your buttons! Do you think I'm going to share you with my cook and fight over you with my maid? No! I'm going to stay. My father will come home — find his desk broken into — his money gone. He'll ring — two rings for the valet. And then he'll send for the sheriff — and I'll tell him everything! He'll have a stroke and die...and there'll be an end to all of us. There'll be peace...and quiet...forever. The coat of arms will be broken. The Count's line will be extinct. And the valet's breed will continue in an orphanage, win triumphs in the gutter, and end in jail!

## *from* **The Duchess of Malfi** (1613)

### (John Webster)

*The Duchess, a woman in her late thirties, is beginning to feel the sour inactivity of age and must come to terms with her own impatience to get on with life and living — in spite of the social customs and conventions of her restrictive society. Here, the Duchess asserts herself to confess her love to Antonio.*

**Duchess:** The misery of us that are born great!
We are forced to woo, because none dare woo us;
And as a tyrant doubles with his words
And fearfully equivocates, so we
Are forced to express our violent passions
In riddles and in dreams, and leave the path
Of simple virtue, which was never made
To seem the thing it is not. Go, go brag
You have left me heartless; mine is in your bosom:
I hope 'twill multiply love there. You do tremble.
Make not your heart so dead a piece of flesh,
To fear more than to love me. Sir, be confident,
What is it distracts you? This is flesh and blood, sir;
'Tis not the figure cut in alabaster
Kneels at my husband's tomb. Awake, awake, man!
I do here put off all vain ceremony
And only do appear to you a young widow
That claims you for her husband; and, like a widow,
I use but half a blush in it.

## *from* **The Way of the World** (1700)

### (William Cosgrove)

*The role of courting in comedy of manners was an elaborate ritual of properly artificial, bright, and vivacious conversation. There was also an opportunity for frivolous reflection that mirrored the manners and mores of the upper classes. Here, Mirabell, a dashing gallant, and Mrs. Millamant, the object of his current affection, share their views on the prospect of their marriage.*

**Mrs. Millamant:** There is not so impudent a thing in nature as the saucy look of an assured man, confident of success. Ah, I'll never marry, unless I am first made sure of my will and pleasure. I'll lie abed in a morning as long as I please. I won't be called names after I'm married. Aye, as wife, spouse, my dear, joy, love, sweetheart, and the rest of the nauseous cant in which men and their wives are so fulsomely familiar. I should also require liberty to pay and receive visits to and from whom I please; to write and receive letters without any interrogatories or wry faces; to wear what I please; and choose conversations with regard only to my own taste. And to have no obligation upon me to converse with wits that I don't like, because they are of some acquaintance. or to be intimate with fools, because they are relations. I shall come to dinner when I please; dine in my dressing gown when I'm out of humor, without giving a reason. To have my closet inviolate; to be sole empress of my tea-table, which no one should pressure to approach without first asking leave. And lastly, wherever I am one shall always knock at the door before entering. These many articles subscribed to, I may in time and by degrees dwindle into a prospective wife.

**Mirabell:** I covenant that your acquaintances be general; that you admit no sworn confidant, or intimate of your own sex. No she-friend to screen her affairs under your countenance, and tempt you to make trial of a mutual secrecy. No decoy-duck to wheedle you a fop scrambling to the play in a mask — then bring you home in a pretended fright, when you think you shall be found out — and rail me for missing the play. Item 1 article, that you continue to like your own face, as long as I shall; and while it passes current with me, that you endeavor not to re-coin it. To which end, together with all vizards for the day, I prohibit all masks for the night, made of oil-skins and I know not what — hog's bones, hare's gall, pig water, and the marrow of roasted cat. I denounce against all strait lacing, squeezing for a shape, till you mold my boy's head like a sugar-loaf. Lastly, to the domination of the tea-table I submit — but with proviso, that you exceed not in your province; but restrain yourself to native and simple tea-table drinks, as tea, chocolate, and coffee. As likewise to genuine and authorized tea-table talk — such as mending of fashions, spoiling reputations, railing at absent friends, and so forth. But that on no account you encroach upon the men's prerogative; and presume to drink healths, or toast fellows. These provisoes admitted, in other things as well I may prove a tractable and complying husband.

# SURVEY OF PERIOD DATES

Here is a brief survey of theatre history dates related to the major movements of literature, theory and performance or production in world drama for your review. The selected dates suggest the approximate time frame for each period indicated and may be a valuable source of information in selecting a playscript for scene study or for potential audition.

| PERIOD | DATES |
|---|---|
| Greek and Roman | c. 525-400 B.C. |
| Medieval | c. 500-1500 |
| Shakespeare, Elizabethan, and Jacobean | c. 1560-1625 |
| Commedia Dell 'Arte | c. 1575-1675 |
| French Neo-Classical | c. 1690-1725 |
| Restoration | c. 1660-1690 |
| 18th/19th Century American and European | c. 1770-1850 |
| Modern | c. 1850-1950 |
| Post-Modern | c. 1950-1970 |
| Absurdism | c. 1950- |
| Contemporary | c. 1970- |

# CHAPTER SIX
# PLAYING MODERN AND
# CONTEMPORARY MONOLOGS

*"Imagination, Industry, and Intelligence — 'The Three I's' —*
*are all indispensable to the actor, but of these three the*
*greatest is, without any doubt, Imagination."*
— Ellen Terry, *Memoirs*

The movement toward modernism in the theatre began c. 1870, and most of the general characteristics associated with this more realistic style of playwriting and performance are attributed to Henrik Ibsen (1828-1906). As the "Father of Modern Drama," Ibsen's primary objective was to write playscripts that were truthful depictions of the world in which he lived; and he thought of himself as one who revealed human nature and society as objectively as possible. A secondary objective of Ibsen was to identify universal themes such as the struggle for integrity or personal values; and the conflict between duty to oneself and the duty to others as a means of expressing the basic dignity of mankind.

In his effort to depict realism through the use of observed facts from daily existence or experience, Ibsen discarded the historical use of the theatrical aside, the classical tragic hero, the Shakespearean soliloquy, and the later period use of direct address to the audience. He also abandoned drawing-room comedies of manner, melodramatic storylines, and spectacle in favor of polite, everyday language and simple action that revealed a character's intention or motivation through rather ordinary stage business and commonplace settings.

It was this direct, objective observation of lived life that helped Ibsen explore a character's personal relationships and subsequent social problems with a more detached, reporter-like, attitude; and to capture recognizable visual portraits of authentic people, places, and even events as if they had been snapped by a hand-held camera. In playing modern monologs, therefore, the actor must keep in mind that the basic principles of realism suggested by Ibsen indicate that a character's stage actions, dialog, and movement are but a picture of reality, not reality itself. Remember that the effort to achieve realistic characterization with only subtlety and suggestion is the primary audition performance goal in playing modern monologs; and that any attempt to startle or to exaggerate in the performance should be avoided as a potential source of distraction and imitation. The actor should insure that there be no theatrical posing or posturing in the audition performance that might interfere with the realistic action or the realistic character portrait being sketched as the playwright has seen it depicted in everyday life.

There is also a conscious attempt made in modern playscripts to give everyday life a sense of dignity and self-importance so that characters may ultimately glimpse their own worth and human value. Because the language of modern playscripts is based upon its usage by ordinary men and women, the dialog is often punctuated with slang, grammatical error, colloquialism, or common vernacular. In addition, fragmented sentences, broken phrases, incomplete thoughts, or even extended moments of contemplation or silence are frequently featured to capture the inherent eloquence of everyday, uncomplicated conversation and communication. Subsequently, it is always the subtext — or the hidden meaning of a character's thought that lies just beneath the surface of the language — which conveys the verbal or emotional tug-of-war between what a character says and what a character actually means.

In playing modern monologs with accuracy and authenticity in terms of capturing a spirit of the present, you must eliminate all extraneous detail in the development of character and sacrifice ornamental trappings like elaborate costumes, makeup, or props in the audition's performance. It is also important to read modern playscripts as if they were novels or short stories, initially sorting out the characters and allowing the story to tell itself in the characters' actions and the narrative rather than in elaborate movement or staging. Such an approach to the audition performance should capture the vivid and relevant speeches, images, and attitudes of the realistic characters being portrayed; and should also provide creative, inventive insights that may reveal the playwright's apparent point of view.

Your basic audition performance blueprint in playing modern monologs depends upon an ability to create the illusion of reality and to convince the spectator that what is seen or heard is honest, spontaneous, natural, and familiar. It is now assumed that an invisible fourth wall exists between actor and audience; and that all action or dialog will be directed to the other actors within the playing space. Remember that there is no attempt made in a modern, realistic audition performance to engage actively with the audience other than to hold their attention and interest as they eavesdrop and witness the resemblance of the character portrait being drawn to real-life role models.

Finally, in playing the modern monologs that follow in this chapter you are reminded to avoid overly precise use of the voice, exaggerated physicalization, and highly theatrical movement or staging. Approach each modern monolog with sensitivity and objectivity; employing a conversational tone of delivery, a relaxed and natural sense of movement, and an energy that suggests singleness of purpose. It may be helpful to integrate the traditional dress of realism — work clothes, leisure shirts, and slacks — or familiar hand props that help to distinguish realistic characters in modern settings — cigarette lighters, toothpicks, and glasses — in the rehearsal period to provide the imaginative spark that illuminates both the character and the selected monolog being performed.

## *from* **Ghosts** (Henrik Ibsen)

*Here is one of Ibsen's earlier achievements in realism, a playscript that explores the issue of heredity and the sins of the father that doom the son. Mrs. Alving, a woman of integrity and strength, has remained with her husband — in spite of his extramarital affairs — for the sake of duty. Sadly, her beloved son has contracted congenital syphilis from the father; and now Mrs. Alving must confront the price paid for duty as she confesses her sacrifice to Pastor Manders.*

**Mrs. Alving:** You have had your say, Mr. Manders, and tomorrow you will be making a public speech in memory of my husband. I shall not speak tomorrow. But now I wish to speak to you for a little, just as you have been speaking to me. In all that you said just now about me and my husband, and about our life together after you had, as you put it, led me back into the path of duty — there was nothing that you knew at first hand. From that moment you never again set foot in our house — you, who had been our daily companion before that. Well — now, Mr. Manders, now I am going to tell you the truth. I had sworn to myself that you should know it one day — you, and you only! The truth is this, that my husband died just as great a profligate as he was before you married us — in his desires at all events. When Oswald was born, I thought I saw a slight improvement. But it didn't last long. And after that I had to fight doubly hard — fight a desperate fight so that no one should know what sort of a man my child's father was. I had borne with it all, though I knew only too well what he indulged in secret, when he was out of the house. But when it came to the point of the scandal coming within our four walls — Yes, here in our own house. It was in there, *(Pointing to the dining room door)* in the dining room that I got the first hint of it. I heard our maid come up from the garden with water for the flowers in the conservatory. Shortly afterwards, I heard my husband come in too. I heard him say something to her in a low voice. And then I heard — *(With a short laugh)* — oh, it rings in my ears still; with its mixture of what was heartbreaking and what was so ridiculous — I heard my servant whisper: "Let me go, Mr. Alving! Let me be!" My husband had his will with the girl — and that intimacy had consequences, Mr. Manders. But it was I that kept him up to the mark when he had his lucid intervals; it was I that had to bear the whole burden of it when he began his excesses again or took to whining about his miserable condition. I had always before me the fear that it was impossible that the truth should not come out and be believed. That is why the orphanage is to exist, to silence all rumors and clear away all doubt. I had another very good reason as well. I did not wish Oswald, my own son, to inherit a penny that belonged to his father. Yes, the sums of money that — year after year — I have given towards this orphanage, make up the amount of property — I have reckoned it carefully — which in the old days made Mr. Alving a catch. That was my purchase money. I don't wish it to pass into Oswald's hands. My son shall have everything from me. I am determined!

## *from* **Long Day's Journey Into Night** (Eugene O'Neill)

*Although written in 1940, this autobiographical playscript was not authorized for performance by the playwright until after his death in 1953. Working primarily in reminiscences that are recalled as part of the family's annual summer retreat to a New England bungalow, O'Neill — speaking through the character Edmund — masterfully draws a sympathetic portrait of his unhappy and troubled family situation. Here, Edmund — suffering from tuberculosis — walks alone on the beach following an argument with his father and expresses his anger and bitterness.*

**Edmund:** To hell with sense! We're all crazy. What do we want with sense? *(He quotes from Dowson sardonically.)*

> "They are not long, the weeping and the laughter,
> Love and desire and hate:
> I think they have no portion in us after
> We pass the gate.
> They are not long, the days of wine and roses:
> Out of a misty dream
> Our path emerges for a while, then closes
> Within a dream."

*(Staring before him)* The fog was where I wanted to be. Halfway down the path you can't see this house. You'd never know it was here. Or any of the other places down the avenue. I couldn't see but a few feet ahead. I didn't meet a soul. Everything looked and sounded unreal. Nothing was what it is. That's what I wanted — to be alone with myself in another world where truth is untrue and life can hide from itself. Out beyond the harbor, where the road runs along the beach, I even lost the feeling of being on land. The fog and the sea seemed part of each other. It was like walking on the bottom of the sea. As if I had drowned long ago. As if I was a ghost belonging to the fog, and the fog was the ghost of the sea. It felt damned peaceful to be nothing more than a ghost within a ghost. *(He sees his father staring at him with mingled worry and irritated disapproval. He grins mockingly.)* Don't look at me as if I'd gone nutty. I'm talking sense. Who wants to see life as it is, if they

145

can help it? It's the three Gorgons in one. You look in their faces and turn to stone. Or it's Pan. You see him and you die — that is, inside you — and have to go on living as a ghost.

## *from* **The Elephant Man** (Bernard Pomerance)

*This drama was suggested by the life of John Merrick, known as "The Elephant Man" because of his grotesque facial and physical deformity. Frederick Treves, a surgeon and lecturer in anatomy at The London Hospital, treated Merrick and became an intimate friend and confidant. In the following lecture, Treves describes Merrick as he remembers their first meeting.*

**Treves:** The most striking feature about him was his enormous head. Its circumference was about that of a man's waist. From the brow there projected a huge bony mass like a loaf, while from the back of his head hung a bag of spongy fungous-looking skin, the surface of which was comparable to brown cauliflower. On the top of the skull were a few long lank hairs. The osseous growth on the forehead, at this stage about the size of a tangerine, almost occluded one eye. From the upper jaw there projected another mass of bone. It protruded from the mouth like a pink stump, turning the upper lip inside out, and making the mouth a wide slobbering aperture. The nose was merely a lump of flesh, only recognizable as a nose from its position. The deformities rendered the face utterly incapable of the expression of any emotion whatsoever. The back was horrible because from it hung, as far down as the middle of the thigh, huge sacklike masses of flesh covered by the same loathsome cauliflower stain. The right arm was of enormous size and shapeless. It suggested but was not elephantiasis, and was overgrown also with pendant masses of the same cauliflower-like skin. The right hand was large and clumsy —a fin or paddle rather than a hand. No distinction existed between the palm and back, the thumb was like a radish, the fingers like thick tuberous roots. As a limb it was useless. The other arm was remarkable by contrast. It was not only normal, but was moreover a delicately shaped limb covered with a fine skin and provided with a beautiful hand which any woman might have envied. From the chest hung a bag of the same repulsive flesh. It was like a dewlap suspended from the neck of a lizard. The lower limbs had the characters of the deformed arm. They were unwieldy, dropsical-looking, and grossly misshapen. There arose from the fungous skin growths a very sickening stench which was hard to tolerate. To add further burden to his trouble, the wretched man when a boy developed hip disease which left him permanently lame, so that he could only walk with a stick. He was thus denied all means of escape from his tormentors.

## *from* **Tango** (Slawomir Mrozek)

*The rebel Arthur lives in appalling disorder and discomfort with his Bohemian family of absurd misfits: a careless mother who sleeps with a vulgar hoodlum, a pathetic father who chooses to ignore the situation in favor of writing avant-garde plays, and a senile grandmother who plays cards incessantly! Arthur tries desperately to bring a sense of order to this chaos — even planning an old-fashioned wedding with his girlfriend — but is rarely successful in any adventure.*

**Arthur:** Marry me! That's the first step. No more promiscuity, no more dolce vita. A real marriage. Not just dropping into city hall between breakfast and lunch. A genuine old-fashioned wedding with an organ playing and bridesmaids marching down the aisle. I'm especially counting on the procession. It will take them by surprise. That's the whole idea. And, from then on, they won't have time to think, to organize resistance and spread defeatism. It's the first shot that counts. Catching them off guard like that, we can force them to accept conventions they'll never break out of again. It's going to be the kind of wedding they'll have to take part in, and on my terms. I'll turn them into a bridal procession, and at long last my father will be forced to button his fly. What do you say? Everything strictly according to the rules. And at the same time you'll be helping all the women in the world. The rebirth of convention will set them free. What used to be the first rule of every encounter between a man and a woman? Conversation. A man couldn't get what he wanted just by making inarticulate sounds. He couldn't just grunt, he had to talk. And while he was talking, you — the woman — sat there demurely, sizing your opponent up. You let him talk and he showed his hand. Listening serenely, you drew up your own order of battle. Observing his tactics, you planned your own accordingly. Free to maneuver, you were always in command of the situation. You had time to think before coming to a decision and you could drag things out as long as you wanted. Even if he gnashed his teeth and secretly wished you in the bottom of hell, you knew he would never dare hit you. Up to the very last minute you could move freely, securely, triumphantly. Once you were engaged, you were safe, and even then traditional avenues of escape were open to you. Such were the blessings of conversation! But nowadays? Nowadays a man doesn't even have to introduce himself — and you will admit it's handy to know who a man is and what he does for a living.

## *from* The Cavern (Jean Anouilh)

*The remarkable and inventive Jean Anouilh likes to draw logical and sensible conclusions from an apparently illogical and inconsistent reality. As an "absurdist," Anouilh seeks to convey a sense of separation, or alienation, that man experiences when he is isolated from the world and from himself. In the following monolog, the playwright has the character Author introduce his latest mysterious story to provoke the spectator to reason and to think about the essential absurdity of life.*

**Author:** The play we are going to perform tonight is one I've never succeeded in writing. I've written a great many other plays which you have been indulgent enough to applaud, for close on thirty years now. *(He waits a second or two for the applause which does not come, then says.)* Thank you. *(He goes straight on, a little vexed.)* But this one, I've never been able to write. Even so, we're going to try to perform it. Yes, I know. You've paid for your seats without knowing that little point. But those of you who aren't satisfied can ask for your money back at the end of the performance. Well, that is, in theory…Because judging from the stampede at the box office these last few days, I think — to be perfectly honest — that the management hasn't quite worked out the exact procedure of reimbursement. Now, we've been practicing for four weeks. You haven't. And it's the audience who makes the play. I've always thought that we ought to rehearse the public and the press as well. We might have fewer flops. Unfortunately…Anyway, tonight's play isn't made. It's in the making. And we have great hopes of you. I can hear somebody whispering that this has already been done by Pirandello. Well, this isn't quite the same thing as you will see, and, furthermore, it only goes to prove that Pirandello had his problems, too. Yes, well now, the last time I spoke to the manager about this idea of giving customers their money back — in view of the unusual nature of our enterprise — he slapped me heartily on the back and he said, "My dear maestro" — he calls me maestro this year because last year I had a success — the years when I have a flop he calls me "dear old darling" — "My dear maestro," he said, "you're too modest. The case won't even arise!" Anyhow, at least I've warned you. This play — had it been a real play — this play was to be called The Cavern. The Cavern to me represents…Well, you'll see. To begin with: the set. I don't like complicated settings much, they always cover up some weakness. "The theatre," said Lope de Vega, "is two boards, two trestles, and a passion." The two boards and the two trestles are easy, you can always find those. But the passion, the true passion which turns every seven or eight hundred individuals into one single attentive being, that's not so easy to come by. Raggedy little shreds of passion, as a rule, tiny trickles which the author, sitting all by himself with his fountain pen, fondly thought of as a deluge. What I really wanted was no scenery at all, just the characters. But, there we are.

### *from* Luther (John Osborne)

*The playwright John Osborne is generally associated with a group of writers known as the "angry young men," who chronicled the disillusionment of post-war years following World War II. But he is also known for the penetrating treatment of the historical times surrounding the 16th-century religious figure Luther. Here, the middle-aged professional shyster John Tetzel addresses the marketplace crowd assembled to receive his "blessing." He, of course, is only interested in hoodwinking the poor and desperate to buy his "holy indulgences."*

**Tetzel:** Are you wondering who I am, or what I am? Is there anyone here among you, any small child, any cripple, or any sick idiot who hasn't heard of me, and doesn't know why I am here? No? No? Well, speak up then if there is? What, no one? Do you all know me then? Do you all know who I am? If it's true, it's very good, and just as it should be. Just as it should be, and no more than that! However, however — just in case — just in case, mind, there is one blind, maimed midget among you today who can't hear, I will open his ears and wash them out with sacred soap for him! And, as for the rest of you, I know I can rely on you all to listen patiently while I instruct him. Is that right? Can I go on? I'm asking you, is that right, can I go on? I say, "Can I go on?" *(Pause)* Thank you. And what is there to tell this blind, maimed midget who's down there somewhere among you? No, don't look around for him, you'll only scare him and then he'll lose his one great chance, and it's not likely to come again, or if it does come, maybe it'll be too late. Well, what's the good news on this bright day? What's the information you want? It's this! Who is this friar with his red cross? Who sent him, and what's he here for? Don't try to work it out for yourself because I'm going to tell you now, this very minute. I am John Tetzel, Dominican, inquisitor, subcommissioner to the Archbishop of Mainz, and what I bring you is indulgences. Indulgences made possible by the red blood of Jesus Christ, and the red cross you see standing up there behind me is the standard of those who carry them. Look at it! Go on, look at it! What else do you see hanging from the red cross? Well, what do they look like? Why, it's the arms of his holiness, because why? Because it's him who sent me here. Yes, my friend, the Pope himself has sent me with indulgences for you! Fine, you say, but what are indulgences? And what are they to me? What are indulgences? They're only the most precious and noble of God's gifts to men, that's all they are! Before God, I tell you I wouldn't swap my privilege at this moment with that of St. Peter in Heaven because I've already saved more souls with my indulgences than he could ever have done with all his sermons!

## *from* **The Typists** (Murray Schisgal)

*The comedies of Murray Schisgal rely heavily upon implausible settings and incongruity to achieve an amusing point of view that provokes mirth and mayhem. The characters in the following monologs are Paul and Sylvia, two typists who work in a small office for an unseen employer. The action is comprised primarily of routine office business until the idle chatter between the two characters takes a serious turn; and each shares a private moment that is deeply affecting.*

**Sylvia:** My family never had money problems. In that respect we were very fortunate. My father made a good living, while he was alive, that is. He passed away when I was seventeen. You could say he and my mother had a fairly happy marriage. At least we never knew when they were angry with one another, and that's a good thing for children. I have a sister. Charlotte. She's older than I am. She's married now and we don't bother much with each other. But when we were younger you wouldn't believe what went on. Every time we quarreled, according to my parents she was right; I was always wrong. She got everything she wanted, no matter what, and I had to be content with the leftovers. It was just unbearable. Anyway, my father was sick for a long time before he passed away. He had this ring, it was a beautiful ring, with a large onyx stone in it, and when I was a girl I used to play with it. I'd close one eye and I'd look inside of it and I'd see hundreds and hundreds of beautiful red and blue stars. My father had always promised me that ring; he always said it belonged to me. I thought for certain he'd give it to me before he passed away, but he didn't say anything about it; not a word. Well, afterward, I saw it. You know where I saw it? On my sister's finger. He had given it to her. Now I don't think that's a background that leaves many possibilities for development. I don't forgive my father; definitely not. And I don't forgive my sister. My mother, whom I now support with my hard work, still says I'm wrong. *(They type; stop suddenly; turn to one another.)*

**Paul:** I was born in a poor section of Brooklyn. My parents were at each other's throat most of the time. It was a miserable childhood. I had no brothers or sisters; there was only the three of us living in this old run-down house, with cats crying and screaming all night in the alley. Why my parents ever got married, I don't know, and why they stayed together for as long as they did I don't know that either. They're separated now. But it doesn't much matter any more. They were as unlike as any two people could be. All my father wanted was to be left alone to smoke his pipe and listen to the radio. My mother — she was a pretty woman, she knew how to dress, all right — she like to go out and enjoy herself. I was stuck between the two of them and they pulled on both sides. I couldn't talk to one without the other accusing me of being ungrateful; I couldn't touch or kiss one of them without being afraid that the other one would see me and there would be a fight. I had to keep my thoughts to myself. I had to grow up wishing for some kind of miracle. I remember coming home from school one afternoon. I must have been twelve or thirteen. There was this man in the living room with my mother. They weren't doing anything; they were just sitting and talking. But I felt that something was going on. I seemed to stop breathing and I ran out of the house and threw up on the curbstone. Later on I swore to myself that I would make a miracle happen; that I wouldn't ever have to be where I didn't want to be and I wouldn't have to do what I didn't want to do; that I could be myself, without being afraid. But it's rough. With a background like mine you're always trying to catch up; it's as if you were born two steps behind the next fellow. *(They type; stop suddenly.)*

# Contemporary Monologs

The common denominator of "current events" or "recent happenings" since c. 1970 is what distinguishes contemporary playscripts from other theatrical periods of history. The immediate appeal of recent or present-day playscripts is that they address issues and themes that sharpen and redefine the meaning of our own daily lives more objectively. Contemporary playscripts are also more concerned with probing beneath the human surface to investigate a character's inner conflicts, hidden desires, or frustrated passions.

The actor who portrays contemporary character portraits is expected to render a truthful depiction of life as it is currently being lived in the description provided by the playscript. This honest, truthful depiction of contemporary life may focus attention on the social forces that help to shape human behavior or may direct attention to commonplace character activities and actions that reveal individual, personal courage. In addressing current events or recent happenings, contemporary playscripts may also reveal characters at odds with present-day customs, laws, or morés; but confronting each apparent obstacle with fierce determination.

Because contemporary playscripts are more firmly rooted in the present tense, any audition performance approach should be even more restrained and subtle than that associated with playing modern monologs. The important point for the actor to remember is that while the contemporary audition performance approach is still detailed and studied — including analysis of the playscript, character building based upon intention or motivation, and interpretation determined by character actions and reactions — the object now is to conceal the basic acting technique and the obvious mechanics of the inventive character portrait so that the performance appears to be natural, spontaneous self-expression. This audition performance approach speaks more directly and immediately to an audience of contemporaries, who should easily recognize and identify both the character and the given circumstances in their own similar lives; or in the personalities and predicaments of their casual acquaintances and intimate friends.

In playing the contemporary monologs that follow in this chapter, you should clearly define the tidbits of character action suggested and concentrate on a single audition performance objective. It is also important to intensify the emotional or intellectual content of each contemporary monolog; and to personalize the action being described as part of each monolog character's imagined life. This illustrative approach to character building — giving a personal life and meaning to the given circumstances, images, and objects associated with the character — should be an essential ingredient in your audition performance blueprint as well.

The creative invention of limited stage business or movement may provide an added audition performance dimension when playing contemporary monologs; but you are reminded that effective and meaningful stage business or movement must be an authentic part of the action(s) described in each selected monolog, and must be an integral part of the character's distinctive personality. Skillful use of limited hand props or occasional pantomime may also enhance your character development and enrich the dynamic portrait being drawn — especially when the use of limited hand props or pantomime clearly delineates a character's attitude or clearly defines a character's personality traits or mannerisms.

Some attention should be paid to each contemporary monolog character's spontaneous responses or reactions as well; and you should not rely too heavily upon stereotypical physical and vocal actions to convey what each monolog character is thinking or anticipating. A good audition performance approach is to think of the contemporary monolog from a non-theatrical perspective — perhaps imagining that the characters and the given circumstances have the same relationship as you might expect to discover in everyday life or in commonplace settings. The non-theatrical perspective in playing contemporary monologs should encourage you to sharpen skills in personal observation and to avoid artifice and superficiality by concentrating on subtle nuances in both voice and body.

Contemporary performance approaches are based upon flesh-and-blood role models, so you should voice the spoken dialog in a more measured, personal tone; and you may even choose to slur syllables or swallow the endings of some words. There may even be nonverbal reactions that help to communicate a character's individual attitude or mood. Movement may be less fluid and graceful than more formal stage practice demands to imaginatively suggest bodily actions of everyday men or women. Alertness to everyday life and to interesting people in all walks of life may also provide the gesture or the mannerism that gives striking individuality and vitality to your audition performance character portrait.

Finally, in playing contemporary monologs it is important in the rehearsal period to pay careful attention to surface details, minor flaws, and simple responses of contemporary characters as potential clues for interpretation in the audition performance. There are, of course, ample opportunities to use one's own individual, unique traits such as comic flair, physique, or vocal quality to give an added dimension of the here-and-now to your contemporary character portrait. The important audition performance principle to keep in mind when playing contemporary monologs, however, is to weave an honest, believable character portrait that any spectator could easily recognize and just as easily identify in their own similar life experiences!

## *from* **I Hate Hamlet** (Paul Rudnick)

*Andrew Rally, a young and successful television actor, has relocated to New York City to perform Shakespeare's* Hamlet. *There is, however, a major complication: Andrew* hates Hamlet! *He is soon visited by the ghost of the legendary Shakespearean actor John Barrymore, who agrees to serve as Andrew's coach after learning of his first ghastly performance.*

**Andrew:** Last night, right from the start, I knew I was bombing. I sounded big and phony, real thee and thou, and then I started rushing it: "Hi, what's new in Denmark?" I just could not connect. I couldn't get a hold of it. And while I'm...babbling, I look out, and there's this guy in the second row, a kid, like sixteen, obviously dragged there. And he's yawning and he's jiggling his legs and reading his program, and I just wanted to say, "Hey, kid, I'm with you, I can't stand this either!" But I couldn't do that, so I just kept feeling worse and worse, just drowning. And I thought, OK, all my questions are answered — I'm not Hamlet, I'm no actor, what am I doing here? And then I get to the soliloquy, the big job, I'm right in the headlights, and I just thought, oh Christ, the hell with it, just do it!

> To be or not to be, that is the question;
> Whether 'tis nobler in the mind to suffer
> The slings and arrows of outrageous fortune,
> Or to take arms against a sea of troubles
> And by opposing, end them.

And I kept going, I finished the speech, and I look out, and there's the kid — and he's listening. The whole audience — complete silence, total focus. And I was Hamlet. And it lasted about ten more seconds, and then I was back in Hell. And I stayed there. But for that one little bit, for that one speech — I got it. I had it. *Hamlet.* And only eight thousand lines left to go!

## *from* **Boy's Life** (Howard Korder)

*Phil, an anxious and nervous self-dramatizer, regularly meets with his college chums to complain about his lack of success in meeting the right girl. His sexual sob stories are legendary to his friends; and usually involve a romantic tragedy that results in high comedy. Here, he shares the latest chapter in his unsuccessful pursuits with his best friend Jack and describes the brief fling he recently had with the equally neurotic Karen.*

**Phil:** I would have destroyed myself for this woman. Gladly. I would have eaten garbage. I would have sliced my wrists open. Under the right circumstances, I mean, if she said, "Hey, Phil, why don't you just cut your wrists open?" Well, come on, but if seriously…We clicked, we connected on so many things, right off the bat, we talked about God for three hours once. I don't know what good it did, but that intensity…and the first time we went to bed, I didn't even touch her. I didn't want to, understand what I'm saying? And you know, I played it very casually, because, all right, I've had some rough experiences, I'm the first to admit, but after a couple of weeks I could feel we were right there, so I laid it down, everything I wanted to tell her, and…and she says to me…she says…"Nobody should ever need another person that badly." Do you believe that? "Nobody should ever…!" What is that? Is that something you saw on TV? I dump my heart on the table, you give me Dr. Joyce Brothers? "Need, need," I'm saying I love you, is that wrong? Is that not allowed anymore? *(Pause. Jack looks at him.)* And so what if I did need her? Is that so bad? All right, crucify me, I needed her! So what! I don't want to be by myself, I'm by myself I feel like I'm going out of my mind, I do. I sit there, I'm thinking forget it, I'm not gonna make it through the next ten seconds. I just can't stand it. But I do, somehow, I get through the ten seconds, but then I have to do it all over again, cause they just keep coming, all these…seconds, floating by, while I'm waiting for something to happen, I don't know what, a car wreck, a nuclear war or something, that sounds awful but at least there'd be this instant when I'd know I was alive. Just once. Cause I look in the mirror, and I can't believe I'm really there. I can't believe that's me. It's like my body, right, is the size of, what, the Statue of Liberty, and I'm inside it, I'm down in one of the legs, this gigantic hairy leg, I'm scraping around inside my own foot like some tiny fetus. And I don't know who I am or where I'm going. And I wish I'd never been born. *(Pause)* Not only that, my hair is falling out, and that really sucks. *(Pause)*

## *from* **Kennedy's Children** (Robert Patrick)

*A smoke-filled New York City bar on Valentine's Day in 1974 brings together a remarkable cast of characters who relive their experiences of the past decade. As each character recalls his or her shattered dream, lost innocence, or disillusionment in America in the post-Camelot era following the assassination of President John F. Kennedy, there is a dark and corrosive glimpse into the tragic lives of "Kennedy's Children."*

**Carla:** I wanted to be a sex goddess. And you can laugh all you want to. The joke is on me, whether you laugh or not. I wanted to be one — one of *them*. They used to laugh at Marilyn when she said she didn't want to be a sex goddess, she wanted to be a human being. And now they laugh at me when I say, "I don't want to be a human being, I want to be a sex goddess." That shows you right there that something has changed, doesn't it? Rita, Ava, Lana, Marlene, Marilyn — I wanted to *be* one of those. I remember the morning my friend came in and told us all that Marilyn had died. And all those boys were stunned — rigid, literally, as they realized what had left us. Like a flame going out, like a moth fluttering away, like the moon not rising full on the proper night …death, bone-white death. I mean, if the world couldn't support Marilyn Monroe, then wasn't something desperately wrong? And we spent the rest of the damned sixties finding out what it was. We were all living together, me and three gay boys that picked me up when I ran away, in this loft on East Fifth Street, before it became dropout heaven — before anyone even said "dropout" — way back even when commune was still a verb. We were all…old movie buffs, sex-mad — you know, the early sixties. And then my friend, this sweet little queen, he came in and he passed out tranquilizers to everyone, and told us all to sit down, and we thought he was just going to tell us there was a Mae West double feature on somewhere, and he said — he said — he said, "Marilyn Monroe died last night." And all the boys were stunned, but I — felt something sudden and cold in my solar plexus, and I knew then what I wanted to do with my life. I wanted to be the next one. I wanted to be the next one to stand radiant and perfected before the race of man, to shed the luminosity of my beloved countenance over the struggles and aspirations of my pitiful subjects. I wanted to give meaning to my own time, to be the unattainable luring love that drives men on, the angel of light, the golden flower, the best of the universe made womankind, the living sacrifice, the end! *(In ecstasy)* Shit!

## *from* Claptrap (Ken Friedman)

*This monolog is an especially informative and entertaining one because it reveals the insanity and insatiable desire that performers have to audition! It is a riveting, riotous look at the madcap actress Tassie as she tells a friend about her most recent audition fiasco, including all of the theatrical rituals any aspiring performer will recognize instantly!*

**Tassie:** My day? You want to hear about my day? No, you don't! Does anyone really give a damn about my day? No! But, you asked! So, OK, I'll tell you. Today, I spent three and a half hours in line waiting for another audition. I know. I know… But, it was for this daring, new avant-garde theatre group that was going to do *The Cherry Orchard* in a totally wild way: Outdoors in a real forest. Yes! And everyone gets to chop down a tree! Hey, I went. And there must have been over a hundred actors in line, several with sharpened axes. Why didn't I think of that? All I had on was a peasant apron, my red babushka, and heavy boots. But, I looked terrific. For what? Because, just as I'm nearing the head of the line; just when I'm up to my ass in emotional borscht; the word came out: *They changed the play!* You heard me. Changed it! Four from the door and it was now an untitled comedy about a vegetable market in Trenton, New Jersey. Is that stupid? But, there were three roles for women. A ghetto teen: tough, but who secretly reads Plato; an aging produce woman who once had an affair with Fidel Castro (remember him?) and an oversexed librarian who loves young boys more than she loves old books. When I read that list, I flipped. I'm right for all of them! But, now I'm at the door and I'm still wearing my damn boots. I'm screwed! "Next!" I go in. "OK, Tassie, do you know the roles that are open? Three women. Good. Honey, relax. Take a few moments…and improvise." "Huh? Improvise what?" "Improvise. We want to see what you can come up with. Be free. Have fun. Enjoy." Have fun? Enjoy? You nitwit! Have you been standing in line since Tuesday? My throat is dry. My hands are wet. And who the hell am I supposed to be? The tomato-selling Cuba-phile, the philosophic juvenile, or the oversexed pedophile? They waited. I waited. And then it happened. I exploded. I burst into the single greatest audition ever given anywhere by anyone! I was all three at once. A Cuban cashier telling an eight year old Plato to shut his damn mouth in the public library! And then I was a New Jersey dictator stealing fruit from an aging teenager who wanted more from life than papayas and apples! And more. And more! I went up, down, in and out and beyond in an incredible torrent of amazingly perfect choices. Weeping, dancing, loving, and walking as three people at once! Acting? Ha! Above acting. Fission, baby! I flared! I seared! I was fire.

And when it was all over I stood panting in a silence that deserves to be called: enchanted. I waited. My head bowed. And finally, one of them, a man who looked sort of worried, said: "Thank you…very…interesting."

Interesting? Is the Venus DeMilo interesting?

"Thank you, uh…Miss Manson. Do you need your picture?"

And so I left. Again. I walked out…But I was great! They may not know it, because they measure me against themselves. But, I know what I did. And so do you. And as of today, I am special! No matter what they say! I mean, what the hell do those murderers know? So, of course, well now I am a little let down. A little depressed. But, I'll be fine. God. So, that was my day. OK, now how the hell was yours?

## *from* **Aunt Dan and Lemon** (Wallace Shawn)

*A rather frail, introspective young recluse named Lemon (alias Leonora) tells us with chilling calm that she admires the Nazis for their lack of hypocrisy and a family friend named Danielle (known as Aunt Dan) for her corrupting moral views. Here, Lemon describes the seductive attraction she first felt as a child when Aunt Dan visited her in a small cottage at the bottom of an old English garden.*

**Lemon:** And then there was a time when Mother stopped reading. I suppose it was like the games, in a way. There was one evening, some evening, which was the very last time she read to us all, but no one remembered that evening or even noticed it. *(Pause)* Well, across the garden from the main house was a little house which was also ours. My father had built it to use as a study, but it turned out that he never went near it. And so, somehow, over the years, little by little, I found that I was moving all of my things from my own room in the main house across the garden to this little house, till finally I asked to have my bed moved as well, and so the little house became mine. And it was in that little house, whenever Aunt Dan came to visit our family, that she and I would have our evening talks, and when I look back on my childhood, it was those talks which I remember more than anything else that ever happened to me. And particularly the talks we had the summer I was eleven years old, which was the last time my parents and Aunt Dan were friends, and Aunt Dan stayed with us for the whole summer, and she came to visit me every night. And in a way it was an amazing thing that a person like Aunt Dan would spend all that time talking to an eleven-year-old child who wasn't even that bright, talking about every complicated subject in the world, but listening to Aunt Dan was the best, the happiest, the most important experience I'd ever had. *(Pause)* Of course, Aunt Dan wasn't really my aunt. She was one of the youngest Americans ever to teach at Oxford — she was just a couple of years older than my parents — and she was my father's best friend, and my mother's too, and she was always at our house, so to me she was an aunt. Aunt Dan. But my mother and father had other friends, and they had their own lives, and they had each other, and they had me. But I had only Aunt Dan. *(Silence)* The days that summer were awful and hot. I would sit in the garden with Aunt Dan and Mother, squinting up at the sun to see if it had made any progress in its journey toward the earth. Then, eventually, I would wolf down some tea and bread and by six o'clock I'd be in my little house, waiting for Aunt Dan to come and visit. Because Aunt Dan didn't spend her evenings talking in the garden with my parents any more. And as I waited, my mind would already be filling with all the things she'd told me, the people she'd described. *(Pause)* Usually there'd still be some light in the sky when I would hear her steps coming up to the little house. And then she would very ceremoniously knock on the door. "Come in!" I'd shout. I'd already be in my pajamas and tucked in under the warm covers. There'd be a moment's pause. And then she'd come in and sit on my bed.

## *from* **Laughing Wild** (Christopher Durang)

*The perils of modern life in urban America are humorously detailed in this extended monolog by The Man, a character whose entire response to life is written on cue cards! The Man used to be a very "negative person," but he has now taken a personality workshop that appears to have turned his life around. Here he describes a recent incident in the local supermarket, and tries to understand a woman's apparently unprovoked act of hostility toward him.*

**Man:** *(Steps closer to the audience.)* I was in the supermarket the other day about to buy some tuna fish when I sensed this very disturbed presence right behind me. There was something about her focus that made it very clear to me that she was a disturbed person. So I thought — well, you should never look at a crazy person directly, so I thought, I'll just keep looking at these tuna fish cans, pretending to be engrossed in whether they're in oil or in water, and the person will then go away. But instead *wham!* she brings her fist down on my head and screams, "Would you move, asshole?!" *(Pause)* Now why did she do that? She hadn't even said, "Would you please move," at some initial point, so I would've known what her problem was. Admittedly I don't always tell people what I want either — like the people in the movie theatres who keep talking, you know, I just give up and resent them — but on the other hand, I don't take my fist and go *wham!* on their heads! I mean, analyzing it, looking at it in a positive light, this woman probably had some really horrible life story that, you know, kind of, explained how she got to this point in time, hitting me in the supermarket. And perhaps if her life — since birth — had been explained to me, I could probably have made some sense out of her action and how she got there. But even with that knowledge — which I didn't have — it was my head she was hitting, and it's just so unfair. It makes me want to never leave my apartment ever ever again. *(Suddenly he closes his eyes and moves his arms in a circular motion around himself, round and round, soothingly.)* I am the predominant source of energy in my life. I let go of the pain from the past. I let go of the pain from the present. In the places in my body where pain lived previously, now there is light and love and joy. *(He opens his eyes again and looks at the audience peacefully and happily.)* That was an affirmation!

## *from* Two (Jim Cartwright)

*The men of Mrs. Iger's dreams are mythical: hordes of robust Roman centurion officers, rock-solid and god-like heroes, and Herculean conquerors! Here she preaches her gospel of "myth men" like an archeologist unearthing a lost species; and delights in the pleasure her dreams of conquest and passion rekindle in her imagination as she sits on a bar stool in an English pub and shares her notion of the "ideal man."*

**Mrs. Iger:** I love big men. Big quiet strong men. That's all I want. I love to tend to them. I like to have grace and flurry around them. I like their temple arms and pillar legs and synagogue chests and big mouth and teeth and tongue like an elephant's ear. And big carved faces like a natural cliff side, and the Roman empire bone work. And you can really dig deep into 'em, can't you? And there's so much. Gargantuan man, like a Roman Empire, with a voice he hardly uses, but when he does it's all rumbling under his breast plate. So big, big hands, big everything! Like sleeping by a mountain side. Carved men. It's a thrill if you see them run, say for a bus, pounding up the pavement. Good big man, thick blood through tubular veins, squirting and washing him out. It must be like a bloody big red cavernous car wash in there, in him, and all his organs and bits hanging from the rib roof, getting a good daily drenching in this good red blood. They are so bloody big you think they'll never die, and that's another reason you want them. Bloody ox men, Hercules, Thor, Chuck Connors, come on, bring your heads down and take from my 'ickle hand. Let me groom and cuddle you. And herd you. Yes, let me gather all you big men of our Isles and herd you up and lead you across America. You myth men. Myth men. Myth men. Big men love ya!

## *from* **Breezeblock Park** (Willy Russell)

*At a family gathering during the Christmas holidays, Sandra shocks her very conservative parents and relatives by announcing that she is pregnant and leaving home to live with her student boyfriend, Tim. Sandra's father lectures Tim on the importance of marriage, and Tim informs the family that Sandra has discovered new interests in her life like art and theatre. This prompts Uncle Ted to tell the sobering story of what happened when he once went to a theatre.*

**Uncle Ted:** Don't talk to me about theatres! I went to one once. 'Ey, John, what was the name of that play, that play I took you an' y' mother to see when it was rainin' in town? Remember? Waitin' for Godot. That was it. I'll tell y' about theatres. We went in to see this thing, it was about these two tramps waitin' for this mate of theirs. Well, I'm not kiddin' you. All this audience were sittin' there waitin' for him as well. I could see straightaway what was gonna happen though. I'd been in there five minutes an' I knew. I opened me programme didn't I, John? An' I looked down the list, y'know where it gives the names of the characters like? An' straightaway I knew, didn't I? His name's not there in the programme y'see, this Godot's. Well, it's common sense, if his name's not in the programme he's never gonna show up. Y' could wait a hundred years an' he'd still never walk onto the bloody stage. But all the rest of these stupid buggers in the place — they didn't have the sense to look in the programme an' work it out for themselves. I slipped out to this cafe next door an' read the paper. I laughed meself silly at the rest of them next door. When our John come out with his mum, I said to him, didn't I, John? I said to him — don't tell me — the Godot feller didn't turn up!

## *from* **The Search for Signs of Intelligent Life in the Universe** (Jane Wagner)

*Originally written as a one-woman tour de force for the comedienne Lily Tomlin — who played all of the roles — this satirical narrative features Trudy, an eccentric and visionary New York bag lady who freely offers her views on the meaning of life, the values of tofu consciousness, Astroturf neckties and aura goggles. Here, Trudy is nervously awaiting the arrival of her friends from outer space — anticipated radiophonically on her umbrella-hat satellite dish!*

163

**Trudy:** Here we are, standing on the corner of
Walk, Don't Walk.
You look away from me, tryin' not to catch my eye,
but you didn't turn fast enough, did you?

You don't like my raspy voice, do you?
I got this raspy voice
'cause I have to yell all the time
'cause nobody around here ever
*Listens* to me.

You don't like that I scratch so much; yes, and excuse me,
I scratch so much
'cause my neurons are
on *fire.*

And I admit my smile is not at all its Pepsodent best
'cause I think my
caps must've somehow got
osteo*porosis.*

And if my eyes seem to be twirling around like fruit flies —
the better to see you with, my dears!

*Look* at me,
you mammalian-brained *lunkheads!*
I'm not just talking to myself. I'm talking to you, too.
And to you
and you
and you
and you and you and you!

I know what you're thinkin'; you're thinkin' I'm crazy.
You think I give a hoot? You people
look at my shopping bags
call me crazy 'cause I save this junk. What should we call the
ones who
*buy* it?

It's my belief we all, at one time or another,
secretly ask ourselves the question,
"Am I crazy?"
In my case, the answer came back: A resounding
Yes!

You're thinkin': How does a person know if they're crazy
or not? Well, sometimes you don't know. Sometimes you
can go through life suspecting you are
but never really knowing for sure. Sometimes you know for sure
'cause you got so many people tellin' you you're crazy
that it's your word against everyone else's.

Another sign is when you see life so clear sometimes
you black out.
This is your typical visionary variety
who has flashes of insight
but can't get anyone to listen to 'em
'cause their insights make 'em sound *so crazy!*

## *from* Eden Creek (Dwight Watson)

*In this poignant monolog, Hattie B. Moore faces a moral dilemma that only adds to the personal complications of her troubled life: as an unwed mother, she has decided to give her child up for adoption. Although her painful decision is neither sweet nor sour, it does prompt her to question her own values — and to reflect on her own need to leave Eden Creek and see the world as she recalls it from an earlier visit to Chicago.*

**Hattie B. Moore:** I was standing by that huge glass tank staring at all those strange fish when a young man, a man I'd seen earlier that day at the Field Museum, struck up a conversation. He was very handsome and very eager to talk. There was just so much to see and so much to talk about, I was delighted when he asked if he could be my escort. He said he had recently been discharged from the military service and that he was taking a few days to see the fair before going to work. We walked and talked for hours. I remember he asked me what I wanted from life. *(Moving to the bed)* I told him I just wanted to travel all over the world and to introduce myself to every human being. *(Extending her hand)* "Hello, I'm Hattie from Eden Creek!" He must've thought that was kinda funny because he began calling me not just Hattie, but Hattie B. Moore. He said that Hattie B. Moore was the name of a beautiful riverboat that carried passengers up and down the lengths of the great Mississippi. And that while I was in Chicago I was to be his Hattie B. Moore. *(Slight pause)* You know, it's funny, because my Mom's maiden name is Moore, and somehow it seemed right that I adopted her maiden name instead of the name of the father who left me.

*from* **Once a Catholic** (Mary O'Malley)

*The convent of Our Lady of Fatima, a grammar school for young girls, prides itself on the tradition of academic excellence and spiritual piety. Today is a celebration of that tradition, and Father Mullarkey has been invited to hear Form Five A's catechism and to address the young girls on the subject of purity.*

**Father Mullarkey:** Now, I want to say a little word to you about the vital importance of purity. You're all getting to be big girls now. Indeed, some of you are bigger than others! Isn't it a great joy to be young and healthy with all your life before you. Sooner or later you might want to share your life with a member of the opposite sex. The best way to find a boyfriend is to join a Catholic Society where you'll have scope for all sorts of social activities. Now when you've met your good Catholic boy and you're getting to know each other he might suggest a bit of a kiss and a cuddle. Well, let him wait! And if he doesn't want to wait let him go. And cuddling and kissing is bound to arouse bad feelings and desires for the intimate union allowed only in matrimony. *(He bangs on the desk.)* The intimate union of the sexes is a sacred act. A duty to be done in a state of grace by a man and his wife and nobody else! So, until the day you kneel at the altar with a bridal veil on your head you must never be left alone in a room with a boyfriend. Or in a field for that matter! Let the two of you go out and about with other young couples to dances and parties and the like. But a particular word of warning about the latter. There's no doubt at all that alcoholic drinks make a party go with a swing. The danger is that after a couple of drinks a boy and a girl are more inclined to take liberties with each other. To indulge in such liberties is sinful. The girl has the special responsibility in the matter because a boy's passions are more readily aroused. God help him! Show your affection by all means. But keep to holding hands with an occasional kiss on the cheek. A Catholic boy, in his heart of hearts, will be impressed by such insistence on perfect chastity. Ask Our Blessed Lady to keep you free from the temptations of the flesh. And make no mistake about it, a passionate kiss on the lips between a boy and a girl is a serious mortal sin. *(He bangs on the desk.)* When you've the wedding ring on your finger you can fire away to your heart's content! Now, has any girl any question she'd like to ask?

## *from* The Marriage of Bette and Boo
(Christopher Durang)

*The genius of Christopher Durang frequently explores the world of the subconscious to reveal the savage reality of a dysfunctional family life. Here, the "perfect marriage" of Bette and Boo has deteriorated into a series of tragic miscarriages for her and chronic drunkenness for him. Matt, their only surviving son, has also fallen victim to the tragic family events; leaving him a shattered, withdrawn young man grotesquely unhappy.*

**Matt:** Eustacia Vye is definitely neurotic. Whether she is psychotic as well is… In *Return of the Native*, Hardy is dealing with some of the emotional, as well as physical dangers in the… One has to be very careful in order to protect oneself from the physical and emotional dangers in the world. One must always try not to live anywhere near a nuclear power plant. One should never walk past a building that may have a sniper on top of it. In the summer one should be on alert against bees and wasps.

As to emotional dangers, one should always try to avoid crazy people, especially in marriage or live-in situations, but in everyday life as well. Although crazy people often mean well, meaning well is not enough. On some level Attila the Hun may have meant well.

Sometimes it is hard to decide if a person is crazy, like Eustacia Vye in *The Return of the Native*, which is the topic of this paper I'm writing. Some people may seem sane at first, and then at some later point turn out to be totally crazy. If you are at dinner with someone who suddenly seems insane, make up some excuse why you must leave dinner immediately. If they don't know you well, you can say you're a doctor and pretend that you just heard your beeper. If the crazy person should call you later, either to express anger at your abrupt leave-taking or to ask for medical advice, claim the connection is bad and hang up! If they call back, I'm afraid you'll have to have your phone number changed again. When you call the phone company to arrange this, if the person on the line seems stupid, hostile or crazy, simply hang up and call the phone company back again. This may be done as many times as necessary *until you get someone sane!* As the phone company has many employees. *(Breathes)* It is difficult to totally protect oneself, of course, and there are many precautions that one thinks of only when it's too late. But, as Virginia Woolf pointed out in *To the Lighthouse,* admittedly in a different context, the attempt is all!

## *from* Good Night Desdemona (Ann Marie MacDonald)

*A fun parody of William Shakespeare's* Romeo and Juliet, *this monolog features a young teacher who magically appears in the playscript to provide advice to the tragic hero and heroine; but not without humorous consequences to herself! Dressed in long johns, Constance is mistaken for a man and subsequently invited to join Mercutio, Tybalt, and Romeo in the baths!*

**Constance:** No, wait! I can't! I had a bath today.
    What's more, I've got a lot of things to do.
       *(Struggling down)*
    I have to buy a lute, a sword, some hose,
    and teach a class or two before it's noon,
    in time to see a man about a horse.
    Thank God they think that I'm a man.
    *(To God)* Thank you. O thank you!
    How long can I avoid their locker room?
    Those guys remind me of the Stratford shows I've seen,
    where each production has a Roman bath:

the scene might be a conference of state,
but steam will rise and billow from the wings,
while full-grown men in Velcro loin-cloths speak,
while snapping towels at each other.
Why is it Juliet's scenes with her Nurse
are never in a sauna. Or *King Lear:*
imagine Goneril and Regan, steaming
as they plot the downfall of their Dad,
while tearing hot wax from each other's legs;
Ophelia, drowning in a whirlpool full
of naked women. Portia, pumping iron —
*(A woman screams within. Male laughter)*
I want to go home. *(On verge of tears)*
I want to see my cats. I want to read
*Jane Eyre* again and never leave the house.
Where's the Fool? Where's the damn Fool?
How come I end up doing all his work?
I should have waited in the wings
for him to leap on stage and stop the fight,
and then I could have pinned him down
and forced him to reveal the Author's name!
The Author — who must know my true identity.
The Author! Who — I have to pee …
There must be a convent around here somewhere!

## *from* Stepping Out (Richard Harris)

*In a local church hall, located in the north of London, a group of middle-aged women — and one reclusive man — meet for their weekly tap dancing class. The instructor, Mavis, is an ex-professional dancer in her early forties; and she has quite a task at hand in trying to rehearse this motley crew for a grand charity show performance!*

**Mavis:** Okay, everyone, let's get on, shall we? It's our first rehearsal, so lots of concentration, yes? *(Indicating)* Rose, Sylvia and Andy — we'll take you three at the back — no, Rose in the middle please. Then we'll have Maxine, Vera, Lynne and Dorothy — spread yourselves out so you can be seen. But come forward a step, you're crowding — and Geoffrey, let's have you at the front, directly in front of Rose.

Okay. So you're standing with your backs to the audience... *(She will demonstrate, turning her back to them.)* Feet apart, and absolutely perfectly still — nothing moving. The curtains or the lights come up or whatever and you stay there, not moving, absolutely static still. For four counts you do absolutely nothing.

On given counts, back line, middle line and Geoffrey turn round and face the front...no, you don't move your feet and so your legs are crossed... From there you bring the right arm up, leaving the left arm down, you lift the hat and you hold it high — yes? On counts three and four, line of four does exactly the same thing but when you turn you leave the right arm down, holding the hat low. Incidentally, there's going to be some fast bouncing around and you might have bust troubles, so wear something good and firm, yes? *(Generally)* Right. We'll have the first four bars and make sure the intro is spot on — it's got to be good, it's got to have panache, it's got to have the three T's. What are the three T's? Tits, teeth, and tonsils. *(Demonstrates)* You smile, you stick your chest out, you look like you're enjoying it... You've only got two T's, haven't you, Geoffrey? Okay, let's have you in your opening positions and we'll try it again. Quick as you can, please Rose, we've got to get through! Dorothy — just a little smaller... Sylvia, can we get rid of the gum? I want to see your teeth, not hear them... All right? And it's five six seven eight... Da da da dada da for nothing. Da da da dada da back line... Da da da dada da middle line... Sway, sway Geoffrey! Okay. I think the problem is that when you turn, some of you are a little off balance. Right, back into position please and we'll do it again — other way round please, Sylvia — and it's five six seven eight... *(Demonstrates.)* Then...shuffle ball change, shuffle ball change shuffle ball change, six tap springs and hold. Right. Now, let's try it to the music!

## *from* **The Sea** (Edward Bond)

*Set in a small English coastal village, the storyline of the playscript is a simple one: A young man named Willy Carson survives a storm at sea when the boat in which he is sailing with his friend sinks in a storm. Later, he meets and falls in love with Rose Jones, the girl to whom his drowned friend was engaged. Beyond this simple storyline, however, is the undercurrent theme of death and madness voiced by the townspeople of the small village. Here, Mrs. Rafi confesses her own human frailty and loneliness in a plaintive cry for happiness and individual fulfillment.*

**Mrs. Rafi:** I'm afraid of getting old. I've always been a forceful woman. I was brought up to be. People expect my class to shout at them. Bully them. They're disappointed if you don't. It gives them something to gossip about in their bars. When they turn you into an eccentric, it's their form of admiration. Sometimes I think I'm like a lighthouse in their world. I give them a sense of order and security. My glares mark out a channel to the safe harbor. I'm so tired of them. I'm tired of being a sideshow in their little world. Nothing else was open to me. If I were a Catholic... *(She looks around)* it's all right, the vicar's gone...I'd have been an abbess. I'd have terrified the nuns. They'd have loved it. Like living next door to the devil. But the grand old faith didn't allow me even that consolation. Of course, I have my theatricals... *(She looks around as before)* yes, the ladies have gone... none of them can act, you know. Oh no, I'm surrounded by mediocrities. A flaming torch and no path to shine on...I'll grow old and shout at them from a wheelchair. That's what they're waiting for. They get their own back for all the years I bullied them. They wheel you where they like. "Take me there." "You went there yesterday. We want to go the other way." "Take me down to the beach. I want to see the sea." "You don't want to see the sea. You saw the sea yesterday. The wind's bad for your head. If you misbehave and catch a cold, we'll shut you up in bed. You'll stay there for good this time." Subtle. Jessica would probably stick matchsticks under my nails. I'll see she's pensioned off. She is one of those ladies who are meant to die alone in a small room. You give up shouting. You close your eyes and the tears dribble down your ugly old face and you can't even wipe it clean —

they won't give you your hanky. "Don't let her have it. She gets into a tizzy and tears it to shreds." There you are: old, ugly, whimpering, dirty, pushed about on wheels and threatened. I can't love them. How could I? But that's a terrible state in which to move toward the end of your life: to have no love. Has anything been worthwhile? No. I've thrown my life away.

*from* **Tracers** (John DiFusco, Vincent Caristi, Richard Chaves, Eric E. Emerson, Rich Gallavan, Merlin Marston, Harry Stephens, and Sheldon Lettich)

*Written collectively by a group of actors who were Vietnam veterans, this playscript is an unsettling and ultimately devastating personal chronicle of the horror and futility of war itself. The storyline, a collage of interrelated scenes and individual monologs, follows the lives of infantry "grunts" from basic training to active duty in Vietnam combat and, finally, to individual realizations of the atrocities which they have witnessed. Here, Dinky Dau recalls his own gut-wrenching memories of the grim battlefield.*

**Dinky Dau:** I remember the sky was overcast. It was hot and muggy. Everyone's fatigues were drenched with sweat. It was late afternoon and we hadn't seen shit all day. I don't know what the hell I was thinking about right then, I guess my mind was just sorta blank at that point. I was so damn worn out — we all were. We'd been humpin' all day. My whole body was achin', I could hardly concentrate on the trail in front of me. The jungle on both sides of us started to get real dense, and the trail started goin' downhill. Then all of a sudden, out of nowhere, there were twelve or maybe thirteen VC, right in front of us. *(SCOOTER suddenly freezes, points ahead. The others crouch down.)* If the main point man hadn't spotted them, they'd have walked right into us. I watched the point man as he raised his weapon. It was like a movie in slow motion. The point man opened up on the first two or three VC. *(SCOOTER opens fire. Music up with gunfire sound effects. The others open fire. All motions are slow and dreamlike.)* I watched the first two or three VC go down, and then I opened up on full automatic. I creamed one of 'em with an entire clip. I watched my bullets as they ripped across his torso. Everybody was up. Everybody was hyper.

Everybody was hittin'. *(He fumbles with his magazine.)* Damn, I wasn't used to reloading. I couldn't get my clip in. Finally, I got it.

## *from* **Rememberin' Stuff** (Eleanor Harder)

*A provocative and yet quite profound view of human nature, this playscript underscores the basic humanity and fragility that emerges when we simply start "rememberin' stuff." The result, of course, is to unearth personal memories and to reveal a telling awareness of our individual capabilities as well as liabilities. The two monologs that follow blend a good helping of strength, will, and spirit of sadder but, hopefully, wiser young men and women.*

**Maxine:** Well, let's see. *(To GROUP and audience.)* Well, uh…I remember that from the time I was real little, I always wanted a baby of my own. And when I was sixteen I got pregnant, and — now I've got one. *(Short uncomfortable pause, then she continues.)* And I remembered thinkin' that if I had a baby, I'd always have somebody to love and somebody who'd love me. Because nobody else had. Not really, y'know? And then, I — I thought everyone would look up to me, think I was special, because I had a kid. *(Sighs.)* Well, I have a kid now, and yeah, I love him and all, and I guess he loves me. But, I don't know, it sure isn't the way I thought it was gonna be. I mean, like the cute cuddly little puppy I had once? Not. Man, I didn't know a baby was so much work! And I worry when he grows up he might not love me anymore, y'know? I mean, some kids don't. *(Shakes head.)* There's so much stuff to worry about! Like, when he's sick and screams all night, and his daddy — hmph! He never comes around or helps or anything. Don't even know where he is now. And I don't know how I'm gonna manage alone. But, hey. *(Motions toward BABY.)* It's not his fault. He's just a little baby. And I do love him. I really do. It's just — well, I remember thinkin' that havin' a kid would make everything all right. Y'know? Change everything. Well, it sure changed everything, but it didn't make everything all right. But *(Shrugs)* you know, maybe nothin' ever does. Make things right, I mean. *(BABY cries. To BABY.)* All right, all right, I'm comin'. *(Goes to carseat and picks up BABY, then turns to GROUP.)* Hey, I gotta go. See you guys around — *(Shrugs)* sometime. Huh?

**Tony:** Yeah, I share an interest. *(To audience)* Share it with a lot of people. Alcohol. So, okay, what's that got to do with the price of beans? Well, 'cause I'm rememberin' stuff — rememberin' when I got busted for drunk driving. Everybody says I was lucky not to get myself killed or kill somebody else. And I know I was lucky 'cause the car was totalled. So, for awhile I got smart and quit driving when I was drinkin'. *(Grins.)* But I was still drinkin'. Y'know, man, I mean — It helps you forget your problems. Well, *(Shrugs)* helped me, anyhow. So, like, I don't remember when I started. I just know I'd drink anything in sight that had alcohol in it, anytime I could find it. Which wasn't hard. Not at my old man's place. Hell, it was easier to find his booze than to find him. So anyhow, now I'm in one of those counseling programs. You know, for *(Makes quotation marks in the air with his fingers)* "Substance abusers." I didn't think alcohol counted as a "substance." I mean, we got pot heads and speedfreaks and you name it in our program. But my counsellors, I don't know, they consider alcohol a substance, and me a substance abuser. Well, actually, my official title is an "alcoholic." Hey, at my age, I got a title already. *(Shrugs.)* It's an okay program. I mean, if it can keep me from windin' up like my old man, who's a real loser, then I'm willin' to give it a try. For awhile, anyhow. You know, see how it goes. I haven't had a drink this time around for three months. Three months and sixteen days, to be exact. So, no big deal, you say, huh? Well, for an "alcoholic substance abuser" it is a big deal, lemme tell ya. *(Nods, as if to himself.)* So, okay, why did I get started drinking in the first place? I don't remember that. I mean, some things you remember, and some things you don't. Right? I've thought about it, but — well, there's this little story I really like. Says a lot, I think. See, there's these two twins, and some dude says to one of 'em. "Hey, Joe, how come you drink?" And Joe says, " 'Cause my old man's an alcoholic." And then this dude asks the other twin, "Hey, Moe, how come you don't drink?" And Moe says, " 'Cause my old man's an alcoholic." *(Chuckles.)* Yeah. I like that one. *(Shrugs.)* So, guess I'm the first twin, huh? *(Shrugs and grins, snaps his finger a couple of times and moves back into GROUP.)*

## *from* **The Road to Mecca** (Athol Fugard)

*Miss Helen, an elderly woman who has spent the years since her husband's death transforming her home in an arid, barren region of South Africa into a museum showplace, now appears unable to care for herself. Her companion and friend, Elsa, is determined that Miss Helen not be committed to a nursing home. In this monolog, Elsa shares a private confession in order to win Miss Helen's confidence.*

**Elsa:** What it all came down to finally was that there were two very different ideas about what was happening, and we discovered it too late. You see, I was in it for keeps, Helen. I knew that we were going to get hurt, that somehow we would all end up being victims of the situation...but I also believed that when the time came to choose I would be the lucky winner, that he would leave his wife and child and go with me. Boy, was I wrong! Ding-dong, wrong-wrong, tolls Elsa's bell at the close of the day!

Defense mechanism. It still hurts. I'm getting impatient for the time when I'll be able to laugh at it all. I mustn't make him sound like a complete bastard. He wasn't without a conscience. Far from it. If anything, it was too big. The end would have been a lot less messy if he'd known how to just walk away and close the door behind him. When finally the time did come, he sat around in pain and torment, crying — God, that was awful! — waiting for me to tell him to go back to his wife and child. Should have seen him, Helen. He came up with postures of despair that would have made Michelangelo jealous. I know it's all wrong to find another person's pain disgusting, but that is what eventually happened. The last time he crucified himself on the sofa in my living room I felt like vomiting. He told me just too often how much he hated himself for hurting me.

I'm all right now. *(Pause)* Do you know what the really big word is, Helen? I had it all wrong. Like most people, I suppose I used to think it was "love." That's the big one all right, and it's quite an event when it comes along. But there's an even bigger one. Trust. And more dangerous. Because that's when you drop your defenses, lay yourself wide open, and if you've made a mistake, you're in big, big trouble. And it hurts like hell. Ever heard the story about the father giving his son his first lesson in business? *(Miss Helen shakes her head.)* I think it's meant to be a joke, so remember to laugh. He puts his little boy high up on something or other and says to him, "Jump. Don't worry, I'll catch you." The child is nervous, of course, but Daddy keeps reassuring him: "I'll catch you." Eventually the little boy works up enough courage and does jump, and Daddy, of course, doesn't make a move to catch him. When the child has stopped crying — because he has hurt himself — the father says: "Your first lesson in business, my son. Don't trust anybody." *(Pause)* If you tell it with a Jewish accent, it's even funnier!

## *from* **Finding the Sun** (Edward Albee)

*Here is a view of passionate innocence in a young boy who is experiencing the first pangs of longing and lust. Sometimes poignant and sometimes perplexing, the young boy's personal courage and perceptive observations are keen indicators of his own rapid progress toward something stronger and more solid than what he has been as an adolescent.*

**Fergus:** *(Comes forward; speaks to the audience.)* If you think it's easy being my age, well…you have another think coming, as they say. A New England boyhood isn't all peaches and cream, maple syrup and russet autumns. I know it sounds pretty good — wealthy mother and all, private school, WASP education, ASP, to be precise. *Are* there any black Anglo-Saxons? It all sounds pretty nice, and it is. I'm not complaining, it's nice…but it isn't always easy. Being corrupted, for example; now, that's important to a young fellow. Whether he takes advantage of it or not. The corrupting influences really should be there; all you should have to do is turn a corner and there you are, all laid out for you, so to speak — fornication, drugs, stealing, whatever; it should *be* there. But if you live in Grovers Corners, or wherever, pop. Fifteen hundred and thirty-three, it isn't too easy to come by. You have to… search it out. Oh, there's the grocer's youngish widow with her blinds always drawn and the come-hither look, and the mildly retarded girl in the ninth grade has some habits would make a pro blush, and the florist with the dyed hair and the funny walk and the mustache for those inclined that way, or at least want to try it. These things are to be had in a small town, but not without the peril of observation and revelation. What's missing, I suppose is…anonymity. And there are, after all, some things we'd rather do in private — at least until we're practiced to do them well. The lack of anonymity: Well, in a small New England town, if your family's been there eight hundred years, or whatever, and you're "gentry," and you're bright, and your mother practically sends out announcements saying you're bright and destined for great things, well, then…it's not the same, as being able to get it all together behind the bard, so to speak, and then coming out all rehearsed and ready. "I hear you're getting all A's, Fergus; good for you!" "Your Mother says you've decided on Harvard, young fella; well, I hope they've decided on you, ha, ha, ha!" Lordy! Even when I was tiny: "Took his first step, did he?" "Potty trained, is he? Good for him!" Royalty must have been worse, or the children of the very famous. I don't even know what I want to do with my life — if I want to do *anything*. If I want to *live* it, even. Do you know what suicide rate has been making the biggest jumps? Kids. Kids my age. I'm not planning to…kill myself or anything. Don't misunderstand me; I'm happy, relatively happy, as I understand the term. It's just that…well, we kids have all sorts of options. You grown-ups aren't the only ones. Think about that. Thank you. *(Bows, moves off.)*

## *from* Angels Fall (Lanford Wilson)

*The scene is a small mission church in a remote part of New Mexico, where a middle-aged college professor named Niles and his lovely wife, Vita, detour unexpectedly after the highway is closed because of a possible accident at a nearby uranium mine. Confined to the sanctuary of the sun-baked mission church with other stranded travellers, the characters begin to reveal their frustrations, fears, and personal crises which have brought them not only to this place but also to turning points in their individual lives.*

**Niles:** No, people are like snowflakes; there's none quite like any other. I'm sure there is no comparison to the deprivation you have lived with and are running from, but the fact is that the ivory tower is a bloody shambles. How can you be in school and not know that? The fact of the graceless routine of my life in academia is being awakened at three in the morning, called to the village morgue to identify the mutilated and alcohol-sodden corpse of the victim of a car crash. The fact is — let go of me — having the brightest light of my fraudulent teaching career quench itself by jumping off the bridge into the bay because in your enlightened age of sexual permissiveness, he was afraid he was sexually deviant. *(Mumbles.)* Ivory tower... There have been, in fact, seven suicides in the past ten years; in fact, one third of my class each year, and of yours, I'm sure if you bothered to look around you, burn themselves out on drugs and overwork and exposure to the pressures of academic life, and are unable to return, probably to their everlasting benefit, if they knew it. Dear God, how can anyone with eyes *(Vita tries to stop him)* — stop that, please — think that we are out of touch with the real world. If that's the real world, I beg to plead very familiar with the real world, thank you. The calumny, Lord! *(Vita tries again.)* Stop touching me, please! What are you trying to do? Make it better? It will not be better, thank you! I won't embarrass you again. You won't have to endure that again. I wish in God's name the door to this building wasn't so heavy so I could slam it!

# Chapter Seven
# Playing "Non-Dramatic" Monologs

*"Love the art in yourself, not yourself in the art."*
— *Stanislavski*

One of the most challenging demands for the actor is to continue to discover imaginative, inventive audition materials that have performance potential. It is not enough, however, to prepare for the audition performance only; time and energy must be set aside for carefully re-reading familiar playscripts, reviewing new playscripts, and searching diligently for memorable "non-dramatic" literature — adapted or edited from sources other than theatre playscripts — that may promote individual performance skills and talents. In order to refresh and refine audition performance self-confidence, the actor should be alert to playing non-dramatic literature designed to build upon the vocal and physical foundation already achieved in playing monologs in the classical, Shakespeare, period, modern, or contemporary style.

With experience and the practical knowledge gained through extensive rehearsals, the actor should be able to identify potential non-dramatic literature that promotes the look and the feel of a personal self-portrait. Begin the search for everyday situations that are familiar and comfortable; and then try to visualize how you might appear as a character in these commonplace episodes. Relying upon casual observation or planned study of everyday situations may provide valuable performance information and insight when selecting non-dramatic materials that are appropriate for your own individual style or unique personality.

The challenge in playing the non-dramatic audition materials that follow in this chapter is to act instinctively; and to make daring choices in the rehearsal period that build moment-to-moment audience anticipation and suspense in seeing and hearing unfamiliar literature in an audition performance. The non-dramatic materials in this chapter are adapted from novels, short stories, poems, narratives and song lyrics. There are also non-dramatic adaptations from personal diaries, original interior monologs from well-known Shakespearean characters, historical speeches, anonymous epigrams from past historical periods, and public addresses.

As part of the initial preparation for playing non-dramatic monologs, you should focus upon the tempo that underscores the attitude or the mood of the individual character speaking for the most immediate, meaningful impact; and assume a performance perspective that suggests only the present moment described in the selected literature. Eliminate all extraneous detail in the development of non-dramatic characters; and sacrifice ornamental trappings like elaborate costumes or hand props that may be distracting. Allow the story being told to tell itself in the dialog, the narrative, and the action being described rather than in highly theatrical accessories. Individuality is still the hallmark of playing non-traditional audition materials, and successful actors should utilize the reservoir of their own life experiences — coupled with creative imagination — to forge an inspired, insightful character portrait that leaves a memorable, unique imprint on the role being played.

Because these audition monologs are not derived from isolated acts or scenes of traditional playscripts — that could be carefully analyzed in some depth before playing the role — it may be necessary with each selection to isolate the central action and the apparent conflict; improvise individual moments of character action; paraphrase lines of description, dialog, or narrative to better understand the context of the given circumstances; and simulate vocal or physical interaction(s) with imaginary characters that may generate inventive stage business. Regardless of the individual performance approach taken, it is important when playing non-traditional materials to compile interior monologs based upon the brief outline of suggested actions or reactions to better understand the motivation or the intention of the character being described.

As you adapt or edit your own imaginative, inventive non-dramatic monologs for potential audition performance, keep in mind that final choices should be appropriate and suitable in terms of your own self-image and professional range of skill and talent. The final choices you make should establish your age, vocal range, movement potential, or physical type; and any personal additions — vocal or physical — should be integrated only if they are truthful in helping to complete the character portrait suggested in each non-dramatic monolog. So, approach the playing of non-dramatic monologs with an illusion of reality that appears to be honest and natural; and allow the character portrait to be shaped by your own lived experiences and documented observations for the fullest expression of believability.

There should also be some attention paid to the inherent dramatic framework suggested in the potential non-dramatic materials as well — especially the possibilities for internal or external conflict, thoughtful point-of-view, unusual given circumstances, or challenging character intention that might lead to a perceptive interpretation and polished audition performance. In addition, you should detail the opportunities presented for movement, search for the bodily actions and gestures that will allow that character to voice meaningful thoughts, and chart vocal or physical changes that appear to take place in the character during the non-dramatic monolog. This studied investigation may provide inventive approaches to characterization; and also help to sketch an imaginative character portrait that is personal and yet profound.

Playing inventive non-dramatic monologs may more easily reveal your own individual performance skills and talents; and also allow you to place a more personal stamp on the audition because of your own intensive and perceptive work in adapting and editing the selected materials for performance. Remember, however, that what is primarily descriptive in non-dramatic literature must become active in the audition performance. Once you have explored the creative possibilities of playing non-dramatic monologs in the audition performance, your theatrical mind should actually become atuned to the empathic identification and genuine response suggested in the words, phrases, and images discovered in all literature!

Once you have begun to explore adapting, editing, and scripting non-dramatic literature for the audition performance, you will no doubt discover that you can actually enhance your reading, comprehension, and interpretation of more traditional playscripts. The only remaining challenge is to move beyond conventional playscripts conveniently used in audition performance, and to begin to visualize all types of literature as potential material for theatrical performance or production. Just remember, however, that in adapting, editing, or scripting non-dramatic character monologs for audition performance to (1) have a beginning, middle, and an end for the selection; (2) reveal character insight and purpose in your cutting; (3) sustain the episode with energetic movement toward a climax; (4) include appropriate introductions and transitions that set the scene and clarify the actions that follow; (5) have a strong sense of the theatrical moment being captured; (6) promote movement opportunities for creative staging; (7) remain faithful to the theme and the author's apparent point of view in the description of action, character, and the given circumstances; (8) meet the time requirements for the audition performance; (9) display the range of your vocal and physical talents; and (10) reveal yourself in an audition performance of honest emotion and intelligence.

## *from* **Anonymous Epigrams** (3rd Century B.C.)

*The following anonymous epigrams — short poems with a satirical point of view — offer universal character portraits of classical figures who expressed heroic thoughts in simple language. The epigrams are often very pointed in their critical commentary; and provide intimate glimpses of the pleasure as well as the pain in the daily lives of individual Athenian citizens and well-known public figures. The themes of the following selected epigrams are concerned with love, life, and death; but there is an ironic detachment in the poems that points to the very personal tragedy of each character that is sincere and sympathetic.*

### Antiphilus of Cyzicus

When I was dead, they gave me a burial.
Now my bones bleach like yellow wheat.
Once I was laid out with due funeral;
Now the iron share ploughs me below.
Stranger, who said that death ended pain,

When even the tomb yields me again?
A vine climbs over me, who once
As many leaves and clusters fed.
Look at me, all —
In earth's narrow bed I lie,
Sorrow of strangers' eyes.

**Poseidippus**

Which way of life should suit a man?
The market sweats him all it can.
Home gives anxieties to bear;
The land is work, the sea is fear;
To travel rich risks loss of all;
To travel poor is unbearable.
Married men have too much care:
But lonely is the bachelor man.
Children make life a mess,
Yet crippled is he childless.
The young are fools; the old weak.
So only two choices to speak:
Either don't be born at all; or
Breathe your last at first bawl!

# Narratives

Narratives like novels, short stories, poems, or song lyrics are particularly effective when adapted for the audition performance because of the thread of action that appears to give each its basic unity. Each separate episode, adventure, description, or story is easily extracted from the longer text for dramatization without sacrificing character, form, or meaning. Narrative adaptations may be extremely valuable in revealing a character's insight or point of view in any given circumstance; and may also highlight fundamental character traits related to physicality, interior psychological state of mind, or self-image.

## *from* **Princess Ida** (W.S. Gilbert)

King Gama's Song

If you give me your attention, I will tell you what I am:
I'm a genuine philanthropist — all other kinds are sham.
Each little fault of temper and each social defect
In my erring fellow-creatures I endeavour to correct.
To all their little weaknesses I open people's eyes;
And little plans to snub the self-sufficient I devise;
I love my fellow-creatures — I do all the good I can —
Yet everybody says I'm such a disagreeable man!
 And I can't think why!

To compliments inflated I've a withering reply;
And vanity I always do my best to mortify;
A charitable action I can skillfully dissect;
And interested motives I'm delighted to detect;
I know everybody's income and what everybody earns;
And I carefully compare it with the income tax returns;
But to benefit humanity however much I plan,
Yet everybody says I'm such a disagreeable man!
 And I can't think why!

I'm sure I'm no ascetic; I'm as pleasant as can be;
You'll always find me ready with a crushing repartee,
I've an irritating chuckle, I've a celebrated sneer,
I've an entertaining snigger, I've a fascinating leer.
To everybody's prejudice I know a thing or two;
I can tell a woman's age in half a minute — and I do.
But although I try to make myself as pleasant as I can,
Yet everybody says I am a disagreeable man!
 And I can't think why!

## *from* **Go Ask Alice** (Anonymous)

December 10

When I bought you, Diary, I was going to write religiously in you every day, but some days nothing worth writing happens and other days I'm too busy or too bored or too angry or too annoyed, or just too me to do anything I don't have to do. I guess I'm a pretty lousy friend — even to you. Anyway, I have just read the stuff I wrote in the last few weeks and I am being drowned in my own tears, suffocated, submerged, inundated, overpowered. They are a lie! A bitter, evil cursed lie! I could never have written things like that! It was another person, someone else! It must have been! It had to be! Someone evil and foul and degenerate wrote in my book, took over my life. Yes, they did, they did! But even as I write I know I am telling even a bigger lie! Or am I? Has my mind been damaged? Was it really just a nightmare and it seems real? I think I've mixed up things which are true and things which are not. All of it couldn't be true. I must be insane.

I have lamented until I am dehydrated, but calling myself a wretched fool, a beggarly, worthless, miserable, paltry, mean, pitiful, unfortunate, woebegone, tormented, afflicted, shabby, disreputable, deplorable human being isn't going to help me either. I have two choices: I must either commit suicide or try to rectify my life by helping others. That is the path I must take, for I cannot bring further disgrace and suffering upon my family. There is nothing more to say, dear Diary, except I love you, and I love life and I love God. Oh, I do. I really do!

## *from* **The Pirates of Penzance** (W.S. Gilbert)

Major-General's Song

I am the very model of a modern Major-General
I've information vegetable, animal, and mineral,
I know the kings of England, and I quote the fights historical,
From Marathon to Waterloo, in order categorical;
I'm very well acquainted too with matters mathematical,
I understand equations, both the simple and quadratical,
About binomial theorem I'm teeming with a lot o' news —

With many cheerful facts about the square of the hypotenuse.
I'm very good at integral and differential calculus,
I know the scientific names of beings animalculous;
In short, in matters vegetable, animal, and mineral,
I am the very model of a modern Major-General.

I know our mythic history, King Arthur's and Sir Caradoc's,
I answer hard acrostics, I've a pretty taste for paradox,
I quote in elegiacs all the crimes of Heliogabalus,
In conics I can floor peculiarities parabolous.
I can tell undoubted Raphaels from Gerard Dows and Zoffanies,
I know the croaking chorus from the *Frogs* of Aristophanes,
Then I can hum a fugue of which I've heard the music's din afore,
And whistle all the airs from that infernal nonsense *Pinafore*.
Then I can write a washing bill in Babylonic cuneiform,
And tell you every detail of Caractacus's uniform;
In short, in matters vegetable, animal, and mineral,
I am the very model of a modern Major-General.

In fact, when I know what is meant by "mamelon" and "ravelin,"
When I can tell at sight a chassepot rifle from a javelin,
When such affairs as sorties and surprises I'm more wary at,
And when I know precisely what is meant by "commissariat,"
When I have learnt what progress has been made in modern gunnery,
When I know more of tactics than a novice in a nunnery:
In short, when I've a smattering of elemental strategy,
You'll say a better Major-Gener*al* has never *sat* a gee —
For my military knowledge, though I'm plucky and adventury,
Has only been brought down to the beginning of the century;
But still in matters vegetable, animal, and mineral,
I am the very model of a modern Major-General.

## *from* **A Bachelor's Complaint** (Anonymous)

As a single man, I have spent a good deal of my time in noting down the infirmities of married people, to console myself for those superior pleasures which they tell me I have lost by remaining as I am. I cannot say that the quarrels of men and their wives ever made any great impression upon me. What oftenest offends me is an error of quite a different description — it is that they are too loving. They carry their preference undisguisedly, they perk it up in the faces of us single people so shamelessly. You cannot be in their company a moment without being made to feel that you are not the object of this preference. It is enough that I know I am not: I do not want this perpetual reminding. Nothing is to me more distasteful than that entire complacency and satisfaction which beam in the countenances of a new-married couple — in that of the lady particularly. It tells you that her lot is disposed of in this world; that you can have no hopes of her. It is true, I have none. Nor wishes either, perhaps. But this is one of those truths which ought to be taken for granted, not expressed. And this is not the worst. If the husband be a man with whom you have lived on a friendly footing before his marriage — look about you — your tenure is precarious. Innumerable are the ways which wives take to insult and worm you out of their husband's confidence. Laughing at all you say with a kind of wonder; as if you were a strange kind of fellow that said good things, *but an oddity!* But what I have spoken of hitherto is nothing to the airs which these creatures give themselves when they come, as they generally do, to have children. When I consider how little of a rarity these children are, I cannot for my life tell what cause for pride there can possibly be in ever having them!

## *from* **The Adventures of Huckleberry Finn**
### (Mark Twain)

I felt good and all washed clean of sin for the first time I had ever felt so in my life, and I knowed I could pray now. But I didn't do it straight off, but laid the paper down and then set there thinking — thinking how good it was all this happened so, and how near I come to being lost and going to hell. And went on thinking. And got to thinking over our trip down the river; and I see Jim before me all the time: in the day and in the nighttime, sometimes in moonlight, sometimes storms, and we a-floating along, talking and singing and laughing. But somehow I couldn't seem to strike no place to harden me against him, but only the other kind. I'd see him standing my watch on top of his'n 'stead of calling me, so I could go on sleeping and see him how glad he was when I came back out of the fog; and when I come to him again in the swamp, up there where the feud was; and such-like times; and would always call me honey, and pet me, and do everything he could think of for me, and how good he always was; and at last I struck the time I saved him by telling the men we had smallpox aboard, and he was so grateful, and said I was the best friend old Jim ever had in the world, and the only one he's got now; and then I happened to look around and see that paper: It was a close place. I took it up, and held it in my hand. I was a-trembling, because I'd got to decide, forever; betwixt two things, and I knowed it. I studies a minute, sort of holding my breath, and then says to myself: "All right, then I'll go to hell" — and then tore it up...

## *from* My Love Is Like to Ice (Edmund Spenser)

My love is like to ice, and I to fire:
How comes it then that this her cold so great
Is not dissolved through my so hot desire,
But harder grows the more I her entreat?
Or how comes it that my exceeding heat
Is not allayed by her heart-frozed cold,
But that I burn much more in boiling sweat,
And feel my flames augmented manifold?
What more miraculous things may be told,
That fire, which all things melts, should harden ice,
And ice, which is congeal'd with senseless cold,
Should kindle fire by wonderful device?
    Such is the power of love in gentle mind,
    That it can alter all the course of kind.

## *from* **The Death of Ivan Ilyich** (Leo Tolstoy)

"Yes, I am making them wretched," he thought. "They are sorry, but it will be better for them when I die." He wished to say this but had not the strength to utter it. "Besides, why speak? I must act," he thought. With a look at his wife he indicated his son and said: "Take him away...sorry for him...sorry for you too." He tried to add, "forgive me," but said "forego" and waved his hand, knowing that He whose understanding mattered most would understand. And suddenly it grew clear to him that what had been oppressing him and would not leave him was all dropping away at once from two sides, from ten sides, and from all sides. He was sorry for them, he must act so as not to hurt them: release them and free himself from these sufferings. He sought his former accustomed fear of death and did not find it. "Where is it? What death?" There was no fear because there was no death. In place of death there was light. "So that's what it is!" he suddenly exclaimed aloud. "What joy!" To him all this happened in a single instant, and the meaning of that instant did not change. For those present his agony continued for another two hours. Something rattled in his throat, his emaciated body twitched, then the gasping and rattle became less and less frequent. "It is finished!" said someone near him. He heard these words and repeated them in his soul. "Death is finished," he said to himself. "It is no more!" He drew in a breath, stopped in the midst of a sigh, stretched out, and died.

## *from* **Of Studies** (Francis Bacon)

Studies serve for delight, for ornament, and for ability. Their chief use for delight is in privateness and retiring; for ornament, is in discourse; and for ability, is in the judgment and the disposition of business. To spend too much time in studies is sloth; to use them too much for ornament is affectation; to make judgment wholly by their rules is the humor of a scholar. Crafty men condemn studies; simple men admire them; and wise men use them. Read not to contradict and confute, nor to believe and take for granted, nor to find talk and discourse, but to weigh and consider. Some books are to be tasted, others to be swallowed, and some few to be chewed and digested: that is, some books are to be read only in parts; others to be read but not curiously, and some few to be read wholly, and with diligence and attention. Reading maketh a full man; conference a ready man; and writing an exact man. And, therefore, if a man write little, he had need have a great memory; if he confer little, he had need have a present wit; and if he read little, he had need have much cunning, to seem to know that he doth not.

## *from* **A Haunted Man** (Charles Dickens)

Everybody said he looked like a haunted man. The extent of my present claim for everybody is, that they were so far right. He did. Who could have seen his hollow cheek; his sunken brilliant eye; his black-attired figure, grim, although well-knit and well-proportioned; his grizzled hair hanging, like tangled seaweed, about his face — as if he had been, through his whole life, a lonely mark for the chafing and beating of the great deep of humanity — but might have said he looked like a haunted man? Who could have observed his manner, taciturn, thoughtful, gloomy, shadowed by habitual reserve, retiring always and jocund never, with a distraught air of reverting to a bygone place and time, or of listening to some old echoes in his mind, but might have said it was the manner of a haunted man? Who could have heard his voice, slow-speaking, deep, and grave, with a natural fulness and melody in it which he seemed to set himself against and stop, but might have said it was the voice of a haunted man? Who that had seen him in his inner chamber, part library and part laboratory — for he was, as the world knew, far and wide, a learned man in chemistry and a teacher on whose lips and hands a crowd of aspiring ears and eyes hung daily — who that had seen him there, upon a winter night, alone, surrounded by his drugs and instruments and books; the shadow of his shaded lamp a monstrous beetle on the wall, motionless among a crow of spectral shapes raised there by the flickering of the fire upon the quaint objects around him; some of these phantoms (the reflection of glass vessels that held liquids), trembling at heart like things that knew his power to uncombine them, and to give back their component parts to fire and vapour; who that had seen him then, his work done, and he pondering in his chair before the rusted grate and red flame, moving his thin mouth as if in speech, but silent as the dead, would not have said that the man seemed haunted and the chamber too?

## *from* **Notes from Underground** (Fyodor Dostoevsky)

The frightened and wounded expression on her face was followed first by a look of sorrowful perplexity. When I began calling myself a scoundrel and thief and my tears flowed (the tirade was accomplished throughout by tears) her whole face worked convulsively. She was on the point of getting up and stopping me; when I finished she took no notice of my shouting: "Why are you here, why don't you go away?" I realized only that it must have been very bitter of me to say all this. Besides, she was crushed, poor girl; she considered herself infinitely beneath me. How could she feel anger and resentment? She suddenly leapt up from her chair with an irresistible impulse and held out her hands, yearning towards me, though still timid and not daring to stir... At this point there was a revulsion in my heart, too. Then she suddenly rushed to me, threw her arms 'round me and burst into tears. I, too, could not restrain myself; and sobbed as I never had before.

## Historical Documents

Historical documents like diaries, letters, public speeches, or addresses are also inventive audition performance materials when edited to isolate the inherent "dramatic elements" necessary for character development. The basic theatricality of historical documents that promote a dramatic conflict or visualize a three-dimensional character portrait that is especially vivid, direct, and immediate in its appeal suggests a dynamic monolog for the audition performance. The use of descriptive language and reflective verbal exchanges are also fundamental ingredients in historical documents that translate easily into memorable audition performance monologs.

## *from* **Thoughts** (Blaise Pascal)

When I consider the short duration of my life, swallowed up in the eternity before and after, the little space which I fill, and even can see, engulfed in the infinite immensity of spaces of which I am ignorant, and which know me not, I am frightened, and am astonished at being here rather than there; for there is no reason why here rather than there, why now rather than then. By whose order and direction have this place and time been allotted to me? Who has put me here? We are fools to depend upon the society of our fellow men. Wretched as we are, powerless as we are, they will not aid us; we shall die alone. We should therefore act as if we were alone, and in that case should we build fine houses? No. We should see the truth without hesitation; and if we refuse it, we show that we value the esteem of men more than the search for truth. How many kingdoms know us not!

## *from* **Letters** (Oscar Wilde)

I suddenly became conscious that someone was looking at me. I turned halfway round and saw him for the first time. When our eyes met, I felt that I was growing pale. A curious sensation of terror came over me. I knew that I had come face to face with someone whose mere personality was so fascinating that, if I allowed it to do so, it would absorb my whole nature, my whole soul. I did not want any external influence in my life. You know how independent I am. I have always been my own master; had at least always been so, till I met him. Then — but I don't know how to explain it to you. Something seemed to tell me that I was on the verge of a terrible crisis in my life. I had a strange feeling that fate had in store for me exquisite joys and exquisite sorrows. I grew afraid and turned to leave the room. It was not conscience that made me do so: it was a sort of cowardice. I take no credit for trying to escape.

Conscience and cowardice are really the same things. But conscience is the trade name of the firm. That is all.

## *from* **A Prayer to Saint Catherine** (Anonymous)

Saint Catherine, Saint Catherine —
Lend me thine aid, and grant that
I may never die an old maid.
A husband, Saint Catherine,
A *good* one, Saint Catherine.

Sweet Saint Catherine,
A husband, Saint Catherine.
Handsome, Saint Catherine,
Rich, Saint Catherine,
*Soon*, Saint Catherine!

## *from* **The Union Address** (Daniel Webster)

When my eyes shall be turned to behold, for the last time, the sun in heaven, may I not see him shining on the broken and dishonored fragments of a once glorious Union; on States dissevered, discordant, belligerent; on a land rent with civil feuds, or drenched, it may be, in fraternal blood! Let their last feeble and lingering glance rather behold the gorgeous ensign of the Republic, now known and honored throughout the earth, still full high advance, its arms and trophies streaming in their original luster, not a stripe erased or polluted, nor a single star obscured, bearing for its motto no such miserable interrogatory as "What is all this worth?" nor those words of delusion and folly, "Liberty first and union afterwards," but everywhere, spread all over in characters of living light, blazing on all its ample folds, as they float over the sea and over the land, and in every wind under the whole heavens, that other sentiment, dear to every true American heart — Liberty and Union, now and forever, one and inseparable!

## *from* **My Mother and God** (Harry Golden)

My mother, I would say, was a primitive woman. She spoke only Yiddish. She could read the prayers out of the book but that was all. She spent all her time cooking, cleaning, sewing; sewing for the family as well as professionally for the neighbors. My mother talked with God all the time, actual conversations. She would send you on an errand and as you were ready to dart off into the crowded, dangerous streets, she turned her face upward and said: "Now see that he's all right." She gave the impression that this was a matter-of-fact relationship, part of the covenant. "In the home that boy is my obligation but once he is out on the street, that is Your department and be sure to see to it."

I do not know of any people less chauvinistic than the Jews. Just imagine, if another race had produced the Ten Commandments, for instance. Think of the place that event would have held in history? But the Jews have always insisted that they had nothing to do with any of these wonderful things. God merely used them to establish His moral code among the peoples of the world. This idea influenced our entire history and every phase of our lives. If a dish happened to turn out well, do you think my mother would take credit for it? Not at all. She said it was an act of God. God helped her cook and sew and clean. And sometimes you have to wonder about it. I am thinking of Mother's potato latkes (pancakes) and holishkas (chopped beef and spices rolled in cabbage leaves and cooked in a sweet-and-sour raisin sauce) and kreplach (small portions of dough folded around chopped beef, boiled, and then dropped into a steaming hot platter of golden chicken soup), and I will say this, "If God did not really help her prepare those dishes (as she claimed), how is it that I haven't been able to find anything equal to them in all these years?" This is the kind of evidence that would even stand up in a court of law!

## *from* **On the Enslavement of Men** (Abraham Lincoln)

That is the issue that will continue in this country when these poor tongues of Judge Douglas and myself shall be silent. It is the eternal struggle between these two principles — right and wrong — throughout the world. They are the two principles that have stood face to face from the beginning of time; and will ever continue to struggle. The one is the common right of humanity, and the other the divine right of kings. It is the same principle in whatever shape it develops itself. It is the same spirit that says, "You toil and work and earn bread, and I'll eat it." No matter in what shape it comes, whether from the mouth of a king who seeks to bestride the people of his own nation and live by the fruit of their labor, or from one race of men as an apology for enslaving another race, it is the same tyrannical principle.

## *from* Civil War Letters (Abraham Lincoln)

Executive Mansion
Washington, 1864
November 21

Mrs. Bixby
Boston, Massachusetts

Dear Madam:

I have been shown in the files of the War Department a statement of the Adjutant-General of Massachusetts that you are the mother of five sons who have died gloriously on the field of battle. I feel how weak and fruitless must be any words of mine which should attempt to beguile you from the grief of a loss so overwhelming. But I cannot refrain from tendering to you the consolation that may be found in the thanks of the republic they died to save. I pray that our Heavenly Father may assuage the anguish of your bereavement, and leave you only the cherished memory of the loved and lost, and the solemn pride that must be yours to have laid so costly a sacrifice upon the altar of freedom.

Yours very sincerely and respectfully,
Abraham Lincoln

## *from* An Address on Dunkirk (Winston Churchill)

We have found it necessary to take measures of increasing stringency, not only against enemy aliens and suspicious characters of other nationalities but also against British subjects who may become a danger or a nuisance should the war be transported to the United Kingdom. I know there are a great many people affected by the orders which we have made who are passionate enemies of Nazi Germany. I am very sorry for them, but we cannot, under the present circumstances, draw all the distinctions we should like to do. If parachute landings were attempted and fierce fights followed, those unfortunate people would be far better out of the way for their own sake as well as ours.

We shall not flag nor fail. We shall go on to the end. We shall fight in France and on the seas and oceans; we shall fight with growing confidence and growing strength in the air. We shall defend our island whatever the cost may be; we shall fight on beaches, landing grounds, in fields, in streets and on the hills. We shall never surrender and even if, which I do not for a moment believe, this island or a large part of it were subjugated and starving, then our empire beyond the seas, armed and guarded by the British Fleet, will carry on the struggle until in God's good time the New World, with all its power and might, sets forth to the liberation and rescue of the Old.

## *from* **A Tribute to Eleanor Roosevelt** (Adlai Stevenson)

She has passed beyond these voices, but our memory and her meaning have not — Eleanor Roosevelt. She was a lady — a lady for all seasons. And, like her husband, she left "a name to shine on the entabulatures of truth — forever." There is, I believe, a legend in the Talmud which tells us that in any period of man's history the heavens themselves are held in place by the virtue, love, and shining integrity of twelve just men. They are completely unaware of this function. They go about their daily work, their humble chores — doctors, teachers, workers, farmers, (never, alas, lawyers, so I understand) just ordinary, devoted citizens — and meanwhile the rooftree of creation is supported by them alone. There are times when nations or movements or great political parties are similarly sustained in their purposes and being by the pervasive, unconscious influence of a few great men and women. Can we doubt that Eleanor Roosevelt had in some measure the keeping of the Party's conscience in her special care? She thought of herself as an ugly duckling, but she walked in beauty in the ghettos of the world; bringing with her the reminder of her beloved St. Francis: "It is in the giving that we receive." And wherever she walked beauty was forever there.

## *from* **Catiline's Defiance** (Ben Jonson)

"Traitor!" I go; but, I return! This — trial!
Here I devote your Senate! I've had wrongs
To stir a fever in the blood of age,
Or make the infant's sinews strong as steel.
This day's the birth of sorrow; this hour's work
Will breed proscriptions! Look to your hearths, my Lords!
For there, henceforth, shall sit, for household gods,
Shapes hot from Tartarus; all shames and crimes;
Wan Treachery, with his thirsty dagger drawn;
Suspicion, poisoning his brother's cup;
Naked Rebellion, with the torch and axe,
Making his wild sport of your blazing thrones;
Till Anarchy comes down on you like night,
And Massacre seals Rome's eternal grave.

## *from* **A Love Letter** (John Keats)

My dearest Girl, I must write you a line or two and see if that will assist in dismissing you from my mind for ever so short a time. Upon my soul I can think of nothing else. My love has made me selfish. I cannot exist without you. I am forgetful of every thing but seeing you again — my life seems to stop there — I see no further. You have absorb'd me. I have a sensation at the present moment as though I was dissolving. I should be exquisitely miserable without the hope of soon seeing you. I should be afraid to separate myself far from you. My sweet Fanny, will your heart never change? My love, will it? I have no limit now to my love — Your note came in just here — I cannot be happier away from you. 'Tis richer than an Argosy of Pearles. Do not threat me even in jest. I have been astonished that men could die martyrs for religion — I have shudder'd at it. I shudder no more. I could be martyr'd for my religion — love is my religion! I could die for that. I could die for you. My creed is love and you are its only tenet. You have ravish'd me away by a power I cannot resist till I saw you; and ever since I have seen you I have endeavoured often to reason against the reasons of my Love. I can do that no more — the pain would be too great. My love is selfish. I cannot breathe without you. Yours for ever,                    John Keats

## *from* **Perils of the Dance** (William Prynne)

Dancing is for the most part attended with many amorous smiles, wanton compliments, unchaste kisses, scurrilous songs and sonnets, effeminate music, lust-provoking attire, ridiculous love-pranks; all which savour only of sensuality, of raging fleshly lusts. Therefore it is wholly to be abandoned of all good Christians. Dancing serves no necessary use, no profitable, laudable, or pious end at all; it issues only from the inbred pravity, vanity, wantonness, incontinency, pride, profaneness, or madness of men's depraved natures. Therefore it must needs be unlawful unto Christians. The way to heaven is too steep, too narrow, for men to dance in and keep revel-rout: No way is large or smooth enough for capering roisters, for jumping, skipping, dancing dames, but that broad, beaten, pleasant road that leads to Hell!

## *from* **Please Hear What I'm Not Saying** (Anonymous)

Diary Entry:

Don't be fooled by me.
Don't be fooled by the face I wear.
For I wear a mask. I wear a thousand masks,
Masks that I'm afraid to take off,
And none of them are me.
I give the impression that I'm secure,
That all is sunny and unruffled with me,
Within as well as without.
But don't believe me, please.

I'm afraid that deep-down I'm nothing,
That I'm just no good, and that you
Will see this and reject me.
So I play my game, my desperate
Pretending game. With a façade of
Assurance without, and a trembling
Child within. And so begins the
Parade of masks, the glittering
But empty parade of masks.

Who am I, you may wonder?
I am someone you know very well.
For I am every man you meet, and
I am every woman you meet.

## *from* **Speech to the Congress** (Davy Crockett)

"On Finances and State Affairs"

Mr. Speaker:
The broken fenced state o' the nation, the broken banks, broken
hearts, and broken pledges o' my brother Congressmen here around me,
has riz the boiler o' my indignation, clar up to the high pressure pinte,
an' therefore I have riz to let off the steam of my hull hog patriotism,
without round-about-ation, and without the trimmins. Whar's all the
honor? No whar! And thar it'll stick! Whar's the state revenue? Every
whar but whar it ought to be!
    Whar's the political honesty o' my feller congressmen? Why, in bank
bills and five acre speeches! Whar's all that patriotism? In slantendicular
slurs, challenges and hair trigger pistols! Whar's all that promises? Every
whar! What in the nation have you done this year? Why, wasted paper
enough to calculate all your political sins upon, and that would take a
sheet for each o' you long as the Mississippi, and as broad as all
Kentucky. You've gone ahead in doin' nothin' backwards, till the hull
nations's done up. You've spouted out a Niagary o' juice, told a hail storm
o' lies, drunk a Lake Superior o' liquor, and all, as you say, for the good
o' the nation; but I say, I swar, for her etarnal bankruptification!
    I move that the only way to save the country is for the hull nest o'
your political weasels to cut stick home instanterly, and leave me to
work Uncle Sam's farm till I restore it to its natural state o' cultivation;
and shake off these state caterpillars o' corruption. Let slick Dan
Webster sittin' there at tother end o' the desk turn Methodist preacher;
let Jack Calhoun settin' right afore him with his hair brushed back in
front like a huckleberry bush in a hurrycane turn to horse-jockey. Let
Harry Clay sittin' thar in the corner with his arms folded about his
middle, like grape vines around a black oak, go back to our old

Kentucky an' improve the breed o' lawyers an' other black sheep. Let old Daddy Quincy Adams sittin' right behind him thar, go home to Massachusetts, an' write political primers for the suckin' politicians; let Jim Buchanan go on home to Pennsylvania, an' smoke long nine, with the Dutchmen. Let Tom Benton, bent like a hickory saplin' with hall rolling, take a roll home an' make candy mint drops for the babies — for they've worked Uncle Sam's farm with the all-scratching harrow o' rascality, 'til it's as gray as a stone fence, as barren as barked clay, and as poor as a turkey fed on gravel stones!

And, to conclude, Mr. Speaker, the nation can no more go ahead under such a state o' things, than a fried eel can swim upon the stream o' a tea kettle; if it can, then take these yar legs for yar hall pillars!

## *from* **Memories** (Boris Pasternak)

You were all my life, my destiny. Then came the war and ruin, too, and for a long time I had no sign, no scrap of news from you. And now I hear your warning voice across the years of grief and pain. At night I read your Testament and rouse myself to life again. I long to be with people, crowds, to share their morning animation; prepared to bring them to their knees, to smash to bits their desolation. And so each morning I run down the stairs, at breakfast, at breakneck speed below. As though this were my first release to long deserted streets in snow. The lights come on in cozy rooms. Men drink their tea, and hurry down to trolley lines. Within an hour you'd hardly recognize the town. The snows are weaving thick and low, their silver nets above the street. Men hurry on to get to work and hardly take their time to eat... My heart goes out to each and all, to everyone who feels he's down. Myself I melt as melts the snow, and as the morning frowns, I frown. As women, children, or even as trees, the nameless are all a part of me. They've won me over, and by that sign I know my sole true victory.

## Additional Dimensions

One of the basic ingredients of a vivid characterization in playing nontraditional audition materials is the actor's creative ability to respond to the images suggested by words and phrases with a voice and a body that is both expressive and exciting. First, however, the actor must conceptualize the images before attempting to visualize the character portrait; and this requires a perceptive and sensitive identification with individual words or phrases in the literature. In the following "breeches roles" — traditional male roles played by *women* wearing men's clothing — from Shakespearean playscripts, respond to the challenge of role-reversal and also discover an inventive performance metaphor that might give added dimension to the character portrait being sketched.

## *from* **Romeo and Juliet** (Prologue)

**Chorus:** Two households, both alike in dignity
In fair Verona, where we lay our scene,
From ancient grudge break to new mutiny,
Where civil blood makes civil hands unclean.
From forth the fatal loins of these two foes
A pair of star-crossed lovers take their life,
Whose misadventured piteous overthrows
Doth with their death bury their parents' strife.
The fearful passage of their death-marked love
And the continuance of their parents' rage —
Which, but their children's end, naught could remove —
Is now the two-hours' traffic of our stage;
The which if you with patient ears attend,
What here shall miss, our toil shall strive to mend.

## *from* **Henry IV, Part II** (Induction)

**Rumor:** Open your ears; for which of you will stop
The vent of hearing when loud Rumor speaks?
I from the orient to the drooping west,
Making the wind my post-horse, still unfold
The acts commenced on this ball of earth.
Upon my tongues continual slanders ride,
The which in every language I pronounce,
Stuffing the ears of men with false reports.
I speak of peace, while covert enmity
Under the smile of safety wounds the world;

And who but Rumor, who but only I,
Make fearful musters and prepared defence
Whiles the big year, swoll'n with some other griefs,
Is thought with child by the stern tyrant war,
And no such matter? Rumor is a pipe
Blown by surmises, Jealousy's conjectures,
And of so easy and so plain a stop
That the blunt monster with uncounted heads,
The still-discordant wav'ring multitude,
Can play upon it. But what need I thus
My well-known body to anatomize
Among my household? Why is Rumor here?
Not a man of them brings any other news
Than they have learnt of me. From Rumor's
They bring smooth comforts false, worse than true wrongs.

## *from* **Henry IV, Part II** (Epilogue)

First my fear, then my curtsy, last my speech.

My fear is your displeasure, my curtsy, my duty;
and my speech to beg your pardons. If you look for
a good speech now, you undo me; for what I have
to say is of mine own making, and what indeed I
should say will, I doubt, prove mine own marring.
But to the purpost, and so to the venture. Be it
known to you, as it is very well, I was lately here in
the end of a displeasing play, to pray your patience
for it, and to promise you a better. I did mean
indeed to pay you with this; which, if like an ill
venture it come unluckily home, I break, and
you, my gentle creditors, lose. Here I promised you
I would be, and here I commit my body to your
mercies. Bate me some, and I will pay you some,
and, as most debtors do, promise you infinitely.

If my tongue cannot entreat you to acquit me,
will you command me to use my legs? And yet
that were but light payment, to dance out of your

debt. But a good conscience will make any possible
satisfaction, and so would I. All the gentlewomen
here have forgiven me; if the gentlemen will not,
then the gentlemen do not agree with the gentlewomen, which was never seen before in such an assembly.
   One word more, I beseech you. If you be not too
much cloyed with fat meat, our humble author
will continue the story with Sir John in it, and
make you merry with fair Katherine of France;
where, for anything I know, Falstaff shall die of a
sweat — unless already a be killed with your hard
opinions. For Oldcastle died a martyr, and this is
not the man. My tongue is weary; when my legs
are too, I will bid you good night, and so kneel
down before you — but, indeed, to pray for the Queen.
*(Dances and then kneels for applause.)*

## Interior Monologs

   A number of experienced actors have either improvised or invented
imaginative theatre games to discover an unwritten interior monolog
based upon spoken dialog or explicit action to better understand the
motivation and the subtext of a character in the given circumstances of
a selected scene or episode. In the process of exploring the interior
monolog these actors may actually begin to give form and shape to an
imaginary character intention or motivation! In the original interior
monologs that follow, the literary author Richard Londraville has
written a number of inventive character speeches related to
Shakespeare's *Hamlet* to voice for the first time their previously secret,
innermost thoughts.

### Ophelia

Bless me padre, for I have not sinned,
or if I have, I know not how. I have,
however, chosen the wrong time to be alive,
for I have lost all patterns upon which
a maid must rely. The time is out of joint,

and I am fouled in forces I cannot
comprehend or control, like a twig of
willow whirled and torn in a mountain stream.

My mother's gone, buried ere I could lisp
her name, a ghost-like woman whom I
construct more from other's tales of her than
from any animate memory. From all
accounts this blest saint might have whispered
counsels more politic than can my brother
or my father. I know they love me well, but
in my heart I feel that they are distracted
by matter beyond my narrow compass.

And what of the young Prince? True, he is
above my station, yet in this wild world
it sometimes seems otherwise. He has oft
spoken to me as if his heart would break
with love, though my father warns me these are
portents instead of a most ordinary
craving. I am too young to discern,
but if Laertes is my exemplar,
my father may be right. My soul is not
in its final form; I need a woman's
voice to school me in such matters, and
the queen is my only model. She also
wishes me well, or thus I am assured,
but seems so like a man in her desires
that I fear her best advice is tainted
with the smell of lust and soiled bed-linen.

So I am alone among them all, and
I sense their infirmities invade me,
weigh me down. My being disintegrates
in the alembic of their frenzies,
and my pleas for help echo unheard.
How is it that I have been so encumbered,

so misled, so abandoned, by these
good folk who professed that they wished
only my perdurable bliss and benefit?


## Polonius

Yes, yes, I knew what they all thought of me:
But when sovereigns change, civil service
changes with them, and all compacts and
agreements must be renegotiated,
though of course we must smile and pretend
that God's universe continues constant.

It is, in fact, demonstrable that
I had every right to expect good treatment
for my long and loyal service, but
knew well enough that expectations
cannot be held in one's hand like coins.

It behooved me, then, to see what the new
man wanted, and to adjust accordingly.
I had my family to think of, a young rake
who thought of nothing but his own pleasure,
and a moony girl to keep chaste and out of
harm's way until some lawful marriage
could be arranged. Those two had no idea
of the balance necessary to tiptoe
between subservience and statesmanship,
but as always with the insensible young,
dwelt only in their own callow appetites.

And the young Prince, what anguish his follies
gave me! What could I do but agree with
his blather and hope that one day his mind
would repair? Is it such a marvel then,
that my language from time to time might

not bestride the summit of eloquence?
I spun the words in my mind, seeking for
a gnomon to free us from his madness.
Do you think I am pleased with my failure?
I did the best I could; I strove to serve
my country and my family in a world
collapsing around my addled gray head.

Whatever my sins, I tried to make all
of these misfits conform to some sense of
decency, to make their wobbly world
spin again somewhere near its axis.
And for this I was denied and reviled:
I understand. It is often the statesman's
mission to be the foil of strewn anger.
I have been used before as whipping boy
by master's wrath with absent enemies.
I have learned to be the brunt of outrage
for these sceptered wardens of my state,
and I have borne their stripes willingly.
But what did I do evil enough to be
thus dispatched by a pretentious, surly
stripling through an embroidered tapestry!

# Humorous Monologs

A final ingredient to consider in playing non-dramatic monologs is the role that topical humor or satire might play in the audition performance. The following narrative selections are representative of the subtle humor that arises from essentially serious author points of view. It is important to peer beneath the obvious broad humor suggested in each selection to catch a glimpse of the significant social or moral theme being expressed.

## *from* **A Modest Proposal** (Jonathan Swift)

The number of souls in this kingdom being usually reckoned one million and a half, of these I calculate there may be about two hundred thousand couples whose wives are breeders; from which number I subtract thirty thousand couples who are able to maintain their own children. But this being granted, there will remain an hundred and seventy thousand breeders. I again subtract fifty thousand for those women who miscarry, or whose children die by accident or disease within the year. There are only remaining an hundred and twenty thousand children of poor parents annually born. The question, therefore, is how this number shall be reared and provided for, which, as I have already said, under the present situation of affairs, is utterly impossible by all the methods hitherto proposed by our government. For we can neither employ them in handicraft or agriculture; and they can very seldom pick up a livelihood by stealing till they arrive at six years old; although, I confess, they learn the rudiments much earlier, during which time they can however be looked upon as probationers.

I shall now, therefore, humbly propose my own thoughts; which I hope will not be liable to the least objection. I have been assured by a very knowing American of my acquaintance in London, that a young healthy child well nursed is at a year old a most delicious, nourishing, and wholesome food; whether stewed, roasted, baked, or boiled. And I make no doubt that it will equally serve in a fricassee or a ragout. I do therefore humbly offer it to public consideration that of the hundred and twenty thousand children, already computed, twenty thousand may be reserved for breed, whereof one fourth part to be males, which is more than we allow to sheep, black cattle, or swine. And my reason is that these children are seldom the fruits of marriage, a circumstance not much regarded by our savages; therefore, one male will be sufficient to serve four females.

That the remaining hundred thousand may at a year be offered in sale to the persons of some quality and fortune through the kingdom; always advising the mother to let them suck plentifully in the last month, so as to render them plump and fat for a good table. A child will make two dishes at an entertainment for friends; and when the family dines alone, the fore or hind quarter will make a reasonable dish; and seasoned with a little pepper or salt will be very good boiled on the fourth day, especially in winter.

I grant that this food will be somewhat dear, and therefore very proper for landlords; who, as they have already devoured most of the parents, seem to have the best title to the children!

## *from* **Ether and Me** (Will Rogers)

This is a day of specializing, especially with the doctors. Say, for instance, there is something the matter with your right eye. You go to a doctor and he tells you, "I am sorry, but I am a left-eye doctor; I make a specialty of left eyes." A doctor that doctors on the upper part of your throat he doesn't even know where the lower part goes to. And the highest priced one of all of them is another bird that just tells you which doctor to go to. He can't cure even corns or open a boil himself. He is a Diagnostician, but he's nothing but a traffic cop, to direct ailing people. The old fashioned doctor didn't pick out a big toe or a left ear to make a life's living on. He picked the whole human frame. No matter what end of you was wrong he had to try to cure you single-handed. Personally, I have always felt that the best doctor in the world is the Veterinarian. He can't ask his patient what is the matter — he's just got to know!

# GLOSSARY OF AUDITION TERMS

**Acting Edition:** Post-production publication of a playscript meant for actors and designers. Includes changes made during the production process, such as character movements and description of setting.

**Artistic Director:** Person who is responsible for all artistic or creative decision-making in the theatre; generally selects playscripts, hires directors, and resident company actors.

**Backstage:** Area immediately behind setting and not visible to audience. (Also called "in-the-wings" or "Off-stage.")

**Beats:** Series of character intentions or objectives. A beat begins when a character's intention begins and ends with its completion.

**Bio:** Actor's abbreviated biography used in printed theatre program.

**Bit:** Small piece of stage business used in blocking.

**Bit Part:** Role with few lines of dialog.

**Blocking:** Planned movement and stage composition developed in rehearsal.

**Business:** Small piece of action used in blocking.

**Callbacks:** Follow-up auditions for a playscript that are held after general auditions or tryouts.

**Call Time:** Expected arrival time at rehearsal, audition, or performance.

**Cameo:** Relatively small but pivotal role.

**Casting Against Type:** Choosing actors who are opposite in age, physique, ethnicity, or attitude from the role(s) described in the playscript.

**Cheat:** Moving one's body or face slightly out toward auditorium house; or slight adjustment in movement in any direction to focus or balance stage picture.

**Closed Audition:** Only actors invited to attend may audition.

**Cold Reading:** Actor is given prepared or "set" speech and asked to perform selection with little or no time for preparation.

**Composite:** Group of photos on single page revealing actor in a variety of poses, expressions, or character attitudes.

**Contact List:** Names, addresses, and phone numbers of cast members, director, and stage management for production.

**Counter:** Moving in opposite direction from another actor to balance stage picture.

**Cross:** Physically moving on stage from one place to another.

**Cue:** Action or dialog that signals next business, dialog, or movement that follows.

**Cue-to-Cue:** Technical rehearsal that only practices entrances/exits and light/sound cues rather than acting the script.

**Directed Reading:** Director may give actor specific instructions in dialog interpretation, movement, and vocal or physical desired responses.

**Doubling:** Common performance practice in which actor plays more than one role in a production.

**Extra (Walk-On):** Small role with no lines of dialog.

**Find the Light:** Locate place on stage where lights have been focused; or place where best available light is located.

**Fourth Wall:** Imaginary wall that separates audience from stage playing area.

**French Scene(s):** Break-down of playscript into smaller scenes for rehearsal.

**General Audition:** Monologs prepared in advance by actor; memorized and blocked to demonstrate individual ability rather than audition for a specific playscript role.

**Give Stage:** Change stage position to permit focus or emphasis on another actor.

**Going Up!:** Forgetting lines of dialog or blocking during the audition or a public performance.

**Heads Up!:** Warning! Piece of scenery, lights, or other objects are falling or being lowered from above.

**Improvisation:** Actor "invents" dialog or physical actions spontaneously to explore characterization and movement.

**Inner Life:** Character's personal philosophy, point of view, and individual personality.

**Inner Monolog:** What the "actor" is thinking as the "character" is speaking.

**Non-Dramatic Literature:** Audition performance materials adapted or edited from sources other than traditional theatre playscripts. Examples may include letters, novels, short stories, poems, narratives, diaries, addresses, song lyrics, or public speeches.

**Non-Traditional Casting:** Casting actors in roles which in past theatre practices might not have been considered appropriate; or "color-blind" with no casting preference to race, gender, or ethnicity.

**Objective Memory:** Actor "re-creates" basic stimuli present in past personal experience(s) and "re-experiences" the stimuli in a similar context for a selected monolog or scene.

**Off Book:** Having lines memorized and able to perform without script in hand.

**Open Audition:** All interested actors, amateur and professional, are encouraged to attend and audition.

**Over Play:** Giving action, dialog, or movement more emphasis or exaggeration than required.

**Performance Metaphor:** Implied performance comparison between the character and something else inventive or imaginative.

**Personality Actor:** Actors who reproduce their natural vocal and physical attributes for every role they perform.

**Pick Up Cues:** Leaving no pause or blank space between previous actor's last line of dialog and beginning of next line of dialog.

**Play Up (Plug or Punch):** Emphasize key line, movement, or stage business for greater significance.

**Pre-Cast:** Choosing actors for specific roles before general audition or tryout period is held publicly.

**Prepared Reading:** Actor generally performs two contrasting, memorized monologs — one or two minutes each — from selected periods of theatre history.

**Presentational Acting:** Actor faces the audience full-front and makes little effort to suggest an illusion of reality.

**Resume:** One-page listing of actor's experience attached to 8 x 10 head shot.

**Show Songs:** Songs written directly for stage performance and revealing complex characterization and highly comic or dramatic content.

**Shtick:** Bit of humorous stage business.

**Sides:** Photocopied pages of selected scenes or individual character speeches to be read at auditions.

**Standard American Speech:** Newscasters' speech; no discernible accent or regionalism and excellent diction.

**Steal:** Actor drawing attention away from a character to whom emphasis would normally be given.

**Substitution (Transfer):** Actor uses specific person from personal life experiences and projects that person's personality onto a character in selected monolog or scene.

**Subtext:** The "hidden meaning" of a character's thought that lies just beneath the surface of the language.

**Tag Line:** Final spoken line of dialog when exiting stage.

**Take Stage:** Actor assumes a more prominent body position or moves to a more prominent stage area to gain focus or emphasis.

**Throw Away:** To deliberately underplay or de-emphasize a line of dialog or stage business to achieve focus or attention elsewhere.

**Top:** Additional emphasis given to a line of dialog or an action that is more emphatic than the line of dialog or stage business that precedes it.

**Type Casting:** Choosing actors who by age, physique, ethnicity, or attitude closely resemble the roles they are to play.

**Typing Out:** Typical musical theatre audition process when actors are lined up and then selected or eliminated simply by physical appearance and type.

# RESOURCE MATERIALS

The following resource materials are highly recommended for the beginning or experienced actor who may wish to become better acquainted with additional audition monologs, "new" playscripts, anthologies, summer job listings, or recent theatre directories. The resource materials are representative of current theatre practice and are especially useful in placing theatre script orders or securing subscriptions for trade magazines or newspapers, theatre performance articles, and acting textbooks.

Actors Theatre of Louisville
316 West Main Street
Louisville, Kentucky 40202

American Conservatory Theatre
450 Geary Street
San Francisco, California 94102

Applause Books
211 West 71st Street
New York, New York 10023

The Arena Stage
6th and M Streets, SW
Washington, D.C. 20024

*Art Search*
Theatre Communications Group
355 Lexington Avenue
New York, New York 10017

*Back Stage*
330 West 42nd Street
New York, New York 10036

Cincinnati Playhouse in the Park
Box 6537
Cincinnati, Ohio 45206

Dallas Theatre Center
3636 Turtle Creek Boulevard
Dallas, Texas 75219

Drama Book Store
723 Seventh Avenue
New York, New York 10019

Drama League
P.O. Box 38771
Los Angeles, California 90038

Dramatic Publishing Company
311 Washington Street
Woodstock, Illinois 60098

Dramatists Play Service
440 Park Avenue South
New York, New York 10016

La Jolla Playhouse
Box 12039
La Jolla, California 92039

The Long Wharf Theatre
222 Sargent Drive
New Haven, Connecticut 06511

Meriwether Publishing, Ltd.
885 Elkton Drive
Colorado Springs, Colorado 80907

*Stage Directions*
3101 Poplarwood Court
Suite 310
Raleigh, North Carolina 27604

Steppenwolf Theatre Company
1650 North Halsted Street
Chicago, Illinois 60657

*Theatre Directory*
Theatre Communications Group
355 Lexington Avenue
New York, New York 10017

Tyrone Guthrie Theatre
725 Vineland Place
Minneapolis, Minnesota 55403

Williamstown Theatre Festival
Box 517
Williamstown, Massachusetts 01267

# ABOUT THE AUTHOR

**Gerald Lee Ratliff** has been an active member of the academic, artistic, and professional community for more than twenty-five years. As author of numerous textbooks, articles, and position papers in literature, dramatic theory, and performance studies he has held national offices as President of the Eastern Communication Association and Theta Alpha Phi. He has also served on the national boards of the Association for Communication Administration, American Council of Academic Deans, International Arts Association, Society of Educators and Scholars, and the National Association of Arts Administrators.

In addition, he was awarded the "Distinguished Service Award" from both the Eastern Communication Association and Theta Alpha Phi; was a Fulbright Scholar to China (1990) and a national delegate of the John F. Kennedy Center for the Performing Arts to Russia (1991). Currently, he is serving as the head of the English and Communication program at the State University of New York, Potsdam.

# Order Form

Meriwether Publishing Ltd.
P.O. Box 7710
Colorado Springs, CO 80933
Telephone: (719) 594-4422
Website: www.meriwetherpublishing.com

*Please send me the following books:*

_____ **The Theatre Audition Book  #BK-B224**　　$16.95
by Gerald Lee Ratliff
*Playing monologs from contemporary, modern,
period and classical plays*

_____ **Playing Contemporary Scenes  #BK-B100**　$16.95
edited by Gerald Lee Ratliff
*Thirty-one famous scenes and how to play them*

_____ **Playing Scenes — A Sourcebook for**　　　$14.95
**Performers  #BK-B109**
by Gerald Lee Ratliff
*How to play great scenes from modern and classical theatre*

_____ **Theatre Alive  #BK-B178**　　　　　　　$29.95
by Dr. Norman A. Bert
*An introductory anthology of world drama*

_____ **One-Act Plays for Acting Students  #BK-B159** $16.95
by Dr. Norman A. Bert
*An anthology of complete one-act plays*

_____ **Theatre Games and Beyond  #BK-B217**　　$16.95
by Amiel Schotz
*A creative approach for performers*

_____ **Multicultural Theatre  #BK-B205**　　　　$15.95
edited by Roger Ellis
*Scenes and monologs by multicultural writers*

These and other fine Meriwether Publishing books are available at
your local bookstore or direct from the publisher. Use the handy
order form on this page.

Name: _____

Organization name: _____

Address: _____

City: _____ State: _____

Zip: _____ Phone: _____

❑ **Check Enclosed**

❑ **Visa or MasterCard #** _____

　　　　　　　　　　　　　　　　　*Expiration*
*Signature:* _____ *Date:* _____
　　　*(required for Visa/MasterCard orders)*

**Colorado Residents:** Please add 3% sales tax.
**Shipping:** Include $2.75 for the first book and 50¢ for each additional book ordered.

❑ *Please send me a copy of your complete catalog of books and plays.*

# Order Form

**Meriwether Publishing Ltd.**
P.O. Box 7710
Colorado Springs, CO 80933
Telephone: (719) 594-4422
Website: www.meriwetherpublishing.com

*Please send me the following books:*

_____ **The Theatre Audition Book  #BK-B224      $16.95**
by Gerald Lee Ratliff
*Playing monologs from contemporary, modern,*
*period and classical plays*

_____ **Playing Contemporary Scenes  #BK-B100  $16.95**
edited by Gerald Lee Ratliff
*Thirty-one famous scenes and how to play them*

_____ **Playing Scenes — A Sourcebook for      $14.95
Performers  #BK-B109**
by Gerald Lee Ratliff
*How to play great scenes from modern and classical theatre*

_____ **Theatre Alive  #BK-B178                     $29.95**
by Dr. Norman A. Bert
*An introductory anthology of world drama*

_____ **One-Act Plays for Acting Students  #BK-B159 $16.95**
by Dr. Norman A. Bert
*An anthology of complete one-act plays*

_____ **Theatre Games and Beyond  #BK-B217        $16.95**
by Amiel Schotz
*A creative approach for performers*

_____ **Multicultural Theatre  #BK-B205            $15.95**
edited by Roger Ellis
*Scenes and monologs by multicultural writers*

**These and other fine Meriwether Publishing books are available at
your local bookstore or direct from the publisher. Use the handy
order form on this page.**

Name: _____

Organization name: _____

Address: _____

City: _____ State: _____

Zip: _____ Phone: _____

❑ **Check Enclosed**

❑ **Visa or MasterCard #** _____

Signature: _____   Expiration
                                          Date: _____
            *(required for Visa/MasterCard orders)*

**Colorado Residents:** Please add 3% sales tax.
**Shipping:** Include $2.75 for the first book and 50¢ for each additional book ordered.

❑ *Please send me a copy of your complete catalog of books and plays.*